WOMAN
AND LABOUR

By

OLIVE SCHREINER

First published in 1911

Read & Co.

Copyright © 2020 Read & Co. History

This edition is published by Read & Co. History,
an imprint of Read & Co.

This book is copyright and may not be reproduced or copied in any
way without the express permission of the publisher in writing.

British Library Cataloguing-in-Publication Data
A catalogue record for this book is available
from the British Library.

Read & Co. is part of Read Books Ltd.
For more information visit
www.readandcobooks.co.uk

"Glory of warrior, glory of orator, glory of song,
Paid with a voice flying by to be lost on an endless sea—
Glory of virtue, to fight, to struggle, to right the wrong—
Nay, but she aim'd not at glory, no lover of glory she:
Give her the glory of going on and still to be."

—TENNYSON

CONTENTS

OLIVE SCHREINER

Olive Schreiner was born on Wittebergen Reserve, Cape Colony (present-day Lesotho) in 1855. After finishing school, she found work as a governess and a schoolteacher, and during her free time began to work on a novel about her experiences in South Africa.

When Schreiner had saved enough money, she travelled to Britain, hoping to become a doctor. She lived in London where she began attending lectures at the Medical School, as well as attending socialist meetings. Schreiner met the publisher George Meredith, who in 1883 published her best-known novel, *Story of an African Farm*. A commercial and critical success, it is now seen as a defining work of early feminism – as is her later work, *Women and Labour* (1911).

Over the rest of her life, Schreiner made the acquaintance of a number of figures in London society, including future Prime Minister William Gladstone. In 1889, she returned to South Africa to be with her family. Her brother, William Schreiner, later became prime minister of Cape Colony. Over the next few years she published two collections of short stories, *Dreams* (1891) and *Dream Life and Real Life* (1893). She also became heavily involved in politics, and was a fierce opponent of racism and imperialism. Her 1897 work *Trooper Peter Halkett of Mashonaland* (1897) was a strong attack on British rule in South Africa.

At the outbreak of the First World War, Schreiner moved back to Britain. Over the next four years she was active in the peace movement and worked closely with organizations such as the Union of Democratic Control and the Non-Conscription Fellowship. She returned to South Africa in of August 1920, and dying following a heart attack later that year.

INTRODUCTION

It is necessary to say a few words to explain this book. The original title of the book was "Musings on Woman and Labour."

It is, what its name implies, a collection of musings on some of the points connected with woman's work.

In my early youth I began a book on Woman. I continued the work till ten years ago. It necessarily touched on most matters in which sex has a part, however incompletely.

It began by tracing the differences of sex function to their earliest appearances in life on the globe; not only as when in the animal world, two amoeboid globules coalesce, and the process of sexual generation almost unconsciously begins; but to its yet more primitive manifestations in plant life. In the first three chapters I traced, as far as I was able, the evolution of sex in different branches of non-human life. Many large facts surprised me in following this line of thought by their bearing on the whole modern sex problem. Such facts as this; that, in the great majority of species on the earth the female form exceeds the male in size and strength and often in predatory instinct; and that sex relationships may assume almost any form on earth as the conditions of life vary; and that, even in their sexual relations towards offspring, those differences which we, conventionally, are apt to suppose are inherent in the paternal or the maternal sex form, are not inherent—as when one studies the lives of certain toads, where the female deposits her eggs in cavities on the back of the male, where the eggs are preserved and hatched; or, of certain sea animals, in which the male carries the young about with him and rears them in a pouch formed of his own substance; and countless other such. And above all, this important fact, which had first impressed me when as a child I wandered alone in the African bush and watched cock-o-veets singing their inter-knit love-songs, and small singing birds building their nests together, and caring for and watching over, not only their young, but each other, and which has powerfully influenced all I have thought and felt on sex matters since;— the fact that, along the line of bird life and among certain of its species sex has attained its highest and aesthetic, and one might almost say intellectual, development on earth: a point of development to which no human race as a whole has yet reached, and which represents the realisation of the highest sexual ideal which haunts humanity.

When these three chapters we ended I went on to deal, as far as possible, with woman's condition in the most primitive, in the savage and in the semi-savage states. I had always been strangely interested from childhood in watching the condition of the native African women in their primitive society about me. When I was eighteen I had a conversation with a Kafir woman still in her untouched primitive condition, a conversation which made a more profound impression on my mind than any but one other incident connected with the position of woman has ever done. She was a woman whom I cannot think of otherwise than as a person of genius. In language more eloquent and intense than I have ever heard from the lips of any other woman, she painted the condition of the women of her race; the labour of women, the anguish of woman as she grew older, and the limitations of her life closed in about her, her sufferings under the condition of polygamy and subjection; all this she painted with a passion and intensity I have not known equalled; and yet, and this was the interesting point, when I went on to question her, combined with a deep and almost fierce bitterness against life and the unseen powers which had shaped woman and her conditions as they were, there was not one word of bitterness against the individual man, nor any will or intention to revolt; rather, there was a stern and almost majestic attitude of acceptance of the inevitable; life and the conditions of her race

12

being what they were. It was this conversation which first forced upon me a truth, which I have since come to regard as almost axiomatic, that, the women of no race or class will ever rise in revolt or attempt to bring about a revolutionary readjustment of their relation to their society, however intense their suffering and however clear their perception of it, while the welfare and persistence of their society requires their submission: that, wherever there is a general attempt on the part of the women of any society to readjust their position in it, a close analysis will always show that the changed or changing conditions of that society have made woman's acquiescence no longer necessary or desirable.

Another point which it was attempted to deal with in this division of the book was the probability, amounting almost to a certainty, that woman's physical suffering and weakness in childbirth and certain other directions was the price which woman has been compelled to pay for the passing of the race from the quadrupedal and four-handed state to the erect; and which was essential if humanity as we know it was to exist (this of course was dealt with by a physiological study of woman's structure); and also, to deal with the highly probable, though unproved and perhaps unprovable, suggestion, that it was largely the necessity which woman was under of bearing her helpless young in her arms while procuring food for them and herself, and of carrying them when escaping from enemies, that led to the entirely erect position being forced on developing humanity.

These and many other points throwing an interesting light on the later development of women (such as the relation between agriculture and the subjection of women) were gone into in this division of the book dealing with primitive and semi-barbarous womanhood.

When this division was ended, I had them type-written, and with the first three chapters bound in one volume about the year 1888; and then went on to work at the last division, which I had already begun.

13

This dealt with what is more popularly known as the women's question: with the causes which in modern European societies are leading women to attempt readjustment in their relation to their social organism; with the direction in which such readjustments are taking place; and with the results which in the future it appears likely such readjustments will produce.

After eleven years, 1899, these chapters were finished and bound in a large volume with the first two divisions. There then only remained to revise the book and write a preface. In addition to the prose argument I had in each chapter one or more allegories; because while it is easy clearly to express abstract thoughts in argumentative prose, whatever emotion those thoughts awaken I have not felt myself able adequately to express except in the other form. (The allegory "Three Dreams in a Desert" which I published about nineteen years ago was taken from this book; and I have felt that perhaps being taken from its context it was not quite clear to every one.) I had also tried throughout to illustrate the subject with exactly those particular facts in the animal and human world, with which I had come into personal contact and which had helped to form the conclusions which were given; as it has always seemed to me that in dealing with sociological questions a knowledge of the exact manner in which any writer has arrived at his view is necessary in measuring its worth. The work had occupied a large part of my life, and I had hoped, whatever its deficiencies, that it might at least stimulate other minds, perhaps more happily situated, to an enlarged study of the question.

In 1899 I was living in Johannesburg, when, owing to ill-health, I was ordered suddenly to spend some time at a lower level. At the end of two months the Boer War broke out. Two days after war was proclaimed I arrived at De Aar on my way back to the Transvaal; but Martial Law had already been proclaimed there, and the military authorities refused to allow my return to my home in Johannesburg and sent me to the Colony; nor was I allowed to send any communication through, to any person, who might have extended some care over my possessions. Some eight months after, when the British troops had taken and entered Johannesburg; a friend, who, being on the British side, had been allowed to go up, wrote me that he had visited my house and found it looted, that all that was of value had been taken or destroyed; that my desk had been forced open and broken up, and its contents set on fire in the centre of the room, so that the roof was blackened over the pile of burnt papers. He added that there was little in the remnants of paper of which I could make any use, but that he had gathered and stored the fragments till such time as I might be allowed to come and see them. I thus knew my book had been destroyed.

Some months later in the war when confined in a little up-country hamlet, many hundreds of miles from the coast and from Johannesburg; with the brunt of the war at that time breaking around us, de Wet having crossed the Orange River and being said to have been within a few miles of us, and the British columns moving hither and thither, I was living in a little house on the outskirts of the village, in a single room, with a stretcher and two packing-cases as furniture, and with my little dog for company. Thirty-six armed African natives were set to guard night and day at the doors and windows of the house; and I was only allowed to go out during certain hours in the middle of the day to fetch water from the fountain, or to buy what I needed, and I was allowed to receive no books, newspapers or magazines. A high barbed wire fence, guarded by armed natives, surrounded the village, through which it would have been death to try to escape. All day the pompoms from the armoured trains, that paraded on the railway line nine miles distant, could be heard at intervals; and at night the talk of the armed natives as they pressed against the windows, and the tramp of the watch with the endless "Who goes there?" as they walked round the wire fence through the long, dark hours, when one was allowed neither to light a candle nor strike a match. When a conflict was fought near by, the dying and wounded were brought in; three men belonging to our little village were led out to execution; death sentences were read in our little market-place; our prison was filled with our fellow-countrymen; and we did not know from hour to hour what the next would bring to any of us. Under these conditions I felt it necessary I should resolutely force my thought at times from the horror of the world around me, to dwell on some abstract question, and it was under these circumstances that this little book was written; being a remembrance mainly drawn from one chapter of the larger book. The armed native guards standing against the uncurtained windows, it was impossible to open the shutters, and the room was therefore always so dark that even the physical act of writing was difficult.

A year and a half after, when the war was over and peace had been proclaimed for above four months, I with difficulty obtained a permit to visit the Transvaal. I found among the burnt fragments the leathern back of my book intact, the front half of the leaves burnt away; the back half of the leaves next to the cover still all there, but so browned and scorched with the flames that they broke as you touched them; and there was nothing left but to destroy it. I even then felt a hope that at some future time I might yet rewrite the entire book. But life is short; and I have found that not only shall I never rewrite the book, but I shall not have the health even to fill out and harmonise this little remembrance from it.

It is therefore with considerable pain that I give out this fragment. I am only comforted by the thought that perhaps, all sincere and earnest search after truth, even where it fails to reach it, yet, often comes so near to it, that other minds more happily situated may be led, by pointing out its very limitations and errors, to obtain a larger view.

I have dared to give this long and very uninteresting explanation, not at all because I have wished by giving the conditions under which this little book was written, to make excuse for any repetitions or lack of literary perfection, for these

16

things matter very little; but, because (and this matters very much) it might lead to misconception on the subject-matter itself if its genesis were not exactly understood.

Not only is this book not a general view of the whole vast body of phenomena connected with woman's position; but it is not even a bird's-eye view of the whole question of woman's relation to labour.

In the original book the matter of the parasitism of woman filled only one chapter out of twelve, and it was mainly from this chapter that this book was drawn. The question of the parasitism of woman is, I think, very vital, very important; it explains many phenomena which nothing else explains; and it will be of increasing importance. But for the moment there are other aspects of woman's relation to labour practically quite as pressing. In the larger book I had devoted one chapter entirely to an examination of the work woman has done and still does in the modern world, and the gigantic evils which arise from the fact that her labour, especially domestic labour, often the most wearisome and unending known to any section of the human race, is not adequately recognised or recompensed. Especially on this point I have feared this book might lead to a misconception, if by its great insistence on the problem of sex parasitism, and the lighter dealing with other aspects, it should lead to the impression that woman's domestic labour at the present day (something quite distinct from, though indirectly connected with, the sexual relation between man and woman) should not be highly and most highly recognised and recompensed. I believe it will be in the future, and then when woman gives up her independent field of labour for domestic or marital duty of any kind, she will not receive her share of the earnings of the man as a more or less eleemosynary benefaction, placing her in a position of subjection, but an equal share, as the fair division, in an equal partnership. (It may be objected that where a man and woman have valued each other sufficiently to select one another from all other humans for a lifelong physical union, it is an impertinence to suppose there could be any necessity to adjust economic relations. In love there is no first nor last! And that the desire of each must be to excel the other in service. That this should be so is true; that it is so now, in the case of union between two perfectly morally developed humans, is also true, and that this condition may in a distant future be almost universal is certainly true. But dealing with this matter as a practical question today, we have to consider not what should be, or what may be, but what, given traditions and institutions of our societies, is, today.) Especially I have feared that the points dealt with in this little book, when taken apart from other aspects of the question, might lead to the conception that it was intended to express the thought, that it was possible or desirable that woman in addition to her child-bearing should take from man his share in the support and care of his offspring or of the woman who fulfilled with regard to himself domestic duties of any kind. In that chapter in the original book devoted to the consideration of man's labour in connection with woman and with his offspring more than one hundred pages were devoted to illustrating how essential to the humanising and civilising of man, and therefore of the whole race, was an increased sense of sexual and paternal responsibility, and an increased justice towards woman as a domestic labourer. In the last half of the same chapter I dealt at great length with what seems to me an even more pressing practical sex question at this moment— man's attitude towards those women who are not engaged in domestic labour; toward that vast and always increasing body of women, who as modern conditions develop are thrown out into the stream of modern economic life to sustain themselves and often others by their own labour; and who yet are there bound hand and foot, not by the intellectual or physical limitations of their nature, but by artificial constrictions and conventions, the remnants of a past condition of society. It is largely this maladjustment, which, deeply studied in all its ramifications, will be found to lie as the taproot and central source of the most terrible of the social diseases that afflict us.

The fact that for equal work equally well performed by a man and by a woman, it is ordained that the woman on the ground of her sex alone shall receive a less recompense, is the nearest approach to a wilful and unqualified "wrong" in the whole relation of woman to society today. That males of enlightenment and equity can for an hour tolerate the existence of this inequality has seemed to me always incomprehensible; and it is only explainable when one regards it as a result of the blinding effects of custom and habit. Personally, I have felt so profoundly on this subject, that this, with one other point connected with woman's sexual relation to man, are the only matters connected with woman's position, in thinking of which I have always felt it necessary almost fiercely to crush down indignation and to restrain it, if I would maintain an impartiality of outlook. I should therefore much regret if the light and passing manner in which this question has been touched on in this little book made it seem of less vital importance than I hold it.

In the last chapter of the original book, the longest, and I believe the most important, I dealt with the problems connected with marriage and the personal relations of men and women in the modern world. In it I tried to give expression to that which I hold to be a great truth, and one on which I should not fear to challenge the verdict of long future generations—that, the direction in which the endeavour of woman to readjust herself to the new conditions of life is leading today, is not towards a greater sexual laxity, or promiscuity, or to an increased self-indulgence, but toward a higher appreciation of the sacredness of all sex relations, and a clearer perception of the sex relation between man and woman as the basis of human society, on whose integrity, beauty and healthfulness depend the health and beauty of human life, as a whole. Above all, that it will lead to a closer, more permanent, more emotionally and intellectually complete and intimate relation between the individual man and woman. And if in the present disco-ordinate transitional stage of our social growth it is found necessary to allow of readjustment by means of divorce, it will not be because such readjustments will be regarded lightly, but rather, as when, in a complex and delicate mechanism moved by a central spring, we allow in the structure for the readjustment and regulation of that spring, because on its absolute perfection of action depends the movement of the whole mechanism. In the last pages of the book, I tried to express what seems to me a most profound truth often overlooked—that as humanity and human societies pass on slowly from their present barbarous and semi-savage condition in matters of sex into a higher, it will be found increasingly, that over and above its function in producing and sending onward the physical stream of life (a function which humanity shares with the most lowly animal and vegetable forms of life, and which even by some noted thinkers of the present day seems to be regarded as its only possible function,) that sex and the sexual relation between man and woman have distinct aesthetic, intellectual, and spiritual functions and ends, apart entirely from physical reproduction. That noble as is the function of the physical reproduction of humanity by the union of man and woman, rightly viewed, that union has in it latent, other, and even higher forms, of creative energy and life-dispensing power, and that its history on earth has only begun. As the first wild rose when it hung from its stem with its centre of stamens and pistils and its single whorl of pale petals, had only begun its course, and was destined, as the ages passed, to develop stamen upon stamen and petal upon petal, till it assumed a hundred forms of joy and beauty.

And, it would indeed almost seem, that, on the path toward the higher development of sexual life on earth, as man has so often had to lead in other paths, that here it is perhaps woman, by reason of those very sexual conditions which in the past have crushed and trammelled her, who is bound to lead the way, and man to follow. So that it may be at last, that sexual love—that tired angel who through the ages has presided over the march

20

of humanity, with distraught eyes, and feather-shafts broken, and wings drabbled in the mires of lust and greed, and golden locks caked over with the dust of injustice and oppression—till those looking at him have sometimes cried in terror, "He is the Evil and not the Good of life!" and have sought, if it were not possible, to exterminate him—shall yet, at last, bathed from the mire and dust of ages in the streams of friendship and freedom, leap upwards, with white wings spread, resplendent in the sunshine of a distant future—the essentially Good and Beautiful of human existence.

I have given this long and very wearisome explanation of the scope and origin of this little book, because I feel that it might lead to grave misunderstanding were it not understood how it came to be written.

I have inscribed it to my friend, Lady Constance Lytton; not because I think it worthy of her, nor yet because of the splendid part she has played in the struggle of the women fighting today in England for certain forms of freedom for all women. It is, if I may be allowed without violating the sanctity of a close personal friendship so to say, because she, with one or two other men and women I have known, have embodied for me the highest ideal of human nature, in which intellectual power and strength of will are combined with an infinite tenderness and a wide human sympathy; a combination which, whether in the person of the man or the woman, is essential to the existence of the fully rounded and harmonised human creature; and which an English woman of genius summed in one line when she cried in her invocation of her great French sister:—

"Thou large-brained woman and large-hearted man!"

One word more I should like to add, as I may not again speak or write on this subject. I should like to say to the men and women of the generations which will come after us—"You will look back at us with astonishment! You will wonder at passionate struggles that accomplished so little; at the, to you, obvious paths to attain our ends which we did not take; at the intolerable evils before which it will seem to you we sat down passive; at the great truths staring us in the face, which we failed to see; at the truths we grasped at, but could never quite get our fingers round. You will marvel at the labour that ended in so little—but, what you will never know is how it was thinking of you and for you, that we struggled as we did and accomplished the little which we have done; that it was in the thought of your larger realisation and fuller life, that we found consolation for the futilities of our own."

"What I aspired to be, and was not, comforts me."

O. S.

CHAPTER I

PARASITISM

In that clamour which has arisen in the modern world, where now this, and then that, is demanded for and by large bodies of modern women, he who listens carefully may detect as a keynote, beneath all the clamour, a demand which may be embodied in such a cry as this: Give us labour and the training which fits for labour! We demand this, not for ourselves alone, but for the race.

If this demand be logically expanded, it will take such form as this: Give us labour! For countless ages, for thousands, millions it may be, we have laboured. When first man wandered, the naked, newly-erected savage, and hunted and fought, we wandered with him: each step of his was ours. Within our bodies we bore the race, on our shoulders we carried it; we sought the roots and plants for its food; and, when man's barbed arrow or hook brought the game, our hands dressed it. Side by side, the savage man and the savage woman, we wandered free together and laboured free together. And we were contented!

Then a change came.

We ceased from our wanderings, and, camping upon one spot of earth, again the labours of life were divided between us. While man went forth to hunt, or to battle with the foe who would have dispossessed us of all, we laboured on the land. We hoed the earth, we reaped the grain, we shaped the dwellings, we wove the clothing, we modelled the earthen vessels and drew the lines upon them, which were humanity's first attempt at domestic art; we studied the properties and uses of plants, and our old women were the first physicians of the race, as, often, its first priests and prophets.

We fed the race at our breast, we bore it on our shoulders; through us it was shaped, fed, and clothed. Labour more toilsome and unending than that of man was ours; yet did we never cry out that it was too heavy for us. While savage man lay in the sunshine on his skins, resting, that he might be fitted for war or the chase, or while he shaped his weapons of death, he ate and drank that which our hands had provided for him; and while we knelt over our grindstone, or hoed in the fields, with one child in our womb, perhaps, and one on our back, toiling till the young body was old before its time—did we ever cry out that the labour allotted to us was too hard for us? Did we not know that the woman who threw down her burden was as a man who cast away his shield in battle—a coward and a traitor to his race? Man fought—that was his work; we fed and nurtured the race—that was ours. We knew that upon our labours, even as upon man's, depended the life and well-being of the people whom we bore. We endured our toil, as man bore his wounds, silently; and we were content.

Then again a change came.

Ages passed, and time was when it was no longer necessary that all men should go to the hunt or the field of war; and when only one in five, or one in ten, or but one in twenty, was needed continually for these labours. Then our fellow-man, having no longer full occupation in his old fields of labour, began to take his share in ours. He too began to cultivate the field, to build the house, to grind the corn (or make his male slaves do it); and the hoe, and the potter's tools, and the thatching-needle, and at last even the grindstones which we first had picked up and smoothed to grind the food for our children, began to pass from our hands into his. The old, sweet life of the open fields was ours no more; we moved within the gates, where the time passes more slowly and the world is sadder than in the air outside; but we had our own work still, and were content.

If, indeed, we might no longer grow the food for our people, we were still its dressers; if we did not always plant and prepare the flax and hemp, we still wove the garments for our race; if we did no longer raise the house walls, the tapestries that covered them were the work of our hands; we brewed the ale, and the simples which were used as medicines we distilled and prescribed; and, close about our feet, from birth to manhood, grew up the children whom we had borne; their voices were always in our ears. At the doors of our houses we sat with our spinning-wheels, and we looked out across the fields that were once ours to labour in—and were contented. Lord's wife, peasant's, or burgher's, we all still had our work to do!

A thousand years ago, had one gone to some great dame, questioning her why she did not go out a-hunting or a-fighting, or enter the great hall to dispense justice and confer upon the making of laws, she would have answered: "Am I a fool that you put to me such questions? Have I not a hundred maidens to keep at work at spinning-wheels and needles? With my own hands daily do I not dispense bread to over a hundred folk? In the great hall go and see the tapestries I with my maidens have created by the labour of years, and which we shall labour over for twenty more, that my children's children may see recorded the great deeds of their forefathers. In my store-room are there not salves and simples, that my own hands have prepared for the healing of my household and the sick in the country round? Ill would it go indeed, if when the folk came home from war and the chase of wild beasts, weary or wounded, they found all the womenfolk gone out a-hunting and a-fighting, and none there to dress their wounds, or prepare their meat, or guide and rule the household! Better far might my lord and his followers come and help us with our work, than that we should go to help them! You are surely bereft of all wit. What becomes of the country if the women forsake their toil?"

And the burgher's wife, asked why she did not go to labour in her husband's workshop, or away into the market-place, or go a-trading to foreign countries, would certainly have answered: "I am too busy to speak with such as you! The bread is in the oven (already I smell it a-burning), the winter is coming on, and my children lack good woollen hose and my husband needs a warm coat. I have six vats of ale all a-brewing, and I have daughters whom I must teach to spin and sew, and the babies are clinging round my knees. And you ask me why I do not go abroad to seek for new labours! Godsooth! Would you have me to leave my household to starve in summer and die of cold in winter, and my children to go untrained, while I gad about to seek for other work? A man must have his belly full and his back covered before all things in life. Who, think you, would spin and bake and brew, and rear and train my babes, if I went abroad? New labour, indeed, when the days are not long enough, and I have to toil far into the night! I have no time to talk with fools! Who will rear and shape the nation if I do not?"

And the young maiden at the cottage door, beside her wheel, asked why she was content and did not seek new fields of labour, would surely have answered: "Go away, I have no time to listen to you. Do you not see that I am spinning here that I too may have a home of my own? I am weaving the linen garments that shall clothe my household in the long years to come! I cannot marry till the chest upstairs be full. You cannot hear it, but as I sit here alone, spinning, far off across the hum of my spinning-wheel I hear the voices of my little unborn children calling to me—'O mother, mother, make haste, that we may be!'—and sometimes, when I seem to be looking out across my wheel into the sunshine, it is the blaze of my own fireside that I see, and the light shines on the faces round it; and I spin on the faster and the steadier when I think of what shall come. Do you ask me why I do not go out and labour in the fields with the lad whom I have chosen? Is his work, then, indeed more needed than mine for the raising of that home that shall be ours? Oh, very hard I will labour, for him and for my children, in the long years to come. But I cannot stop to talk to you now. Far off, over the hum of my spinning-wheel, I hear the voices of my children calling, and I must hurry on. Do you ask me why I do not seek for labour whose hands are full to bursting? Who will give folk to the nation if I do not?"

Such would have been our answer in Europe in the ages of the past, if asked the question why we were contented with our field of labour and sought no other. Man had his work; we had ours. We knew that we upbore our world on our shoulders; and that through the labour of our hands it was sustained and strengthened—and we were contented.

But now, again a change has come.

Something that is entirely new has entered into the field of human labour, and left nothing as it was.

In man's fields of toil, change has accomplished, and is yet more quickly accomplishing, itself.

On lands where once fifty men and youths toiled with their cattle, today one steam-plough, guided by but two pair of hands, passes swiftly; and an automatic reaper in one day reaps and binds and prepares for the garner the produce of fields it would have taken a hundred strong male arms to harvest in the past. The iron tools and weapons, only one of which it took an ancient father of our race long months of stern exertion to extract from ore and bring to shape and temper, are now poured forth by steam-driven machinery as a millpond pours forth its water; and even in war, the male's ancient and especial field of labour, a complete reversal of the ancient order has taken place. Time was when the size and strength of the muscles in a man's legs and arms, and the strength and size of his body, largely determined his fighting powers, and an Achilles or a Richard Coeur de Lion, armed only with his spear or battle-axe, made a host fly before him; today the puniest mannikin behind a modern Maxim gun may mow down in perfect safety a phalanx of heroes whose legs and arms and physical powers a Greek god might have envied, but who, having not the modern machinery of war, fall powerless. The day of the primary import to humanity of

27

the strength in man's extensor and flexor muscles, whether in labours of war or of peace, is gone by for ever; and the day of the all-importance of the culture and activity of man's brain and nerve has already come.

The brain of one consumptive German chemist, who in his laboratory compounds a new explosive, has more effect upon the wars of the modern peoples than ten thousand soldierly legs and arms; and the man who invents one new labour-saving machine may, through the cerebration of a few days, have performed the labour it would otherwise have taken hundreds of thousands of his lusty fellows decades to accomplish.

Year by year, month by month, and almost hour by hour, this change is increasingly showing itself in the field of the modern labour; and crude muscular force, whether in man or beast, sinks continually in its value in the world of human toil; while intellectual power, virility, and activity, and that culture which leads to the mastery of the inanimate forces of nature, to the invention of machinery, and to that delicate manipulative skill often required in guiding it, becomes ever of greater and greater importance to the race. Already today we tremble on the verge of a discovery, which may come tomorrow or the next day, when, through the attainment of a simple and cheap method of controlling some widely diffused, everywhere accessible, natural force (such, for instance, as the force of the great tidal wave) there will at once and for ever pass away even that comparatively small value which still, in our present stage of material civilisation, clings to the expenditure of mere crude, mechanical, human energy; and the creature, however physically powerful, who can merely pull, push, and lift, much after the manner of a machine, will have no further value in the field of human labour.

Therefore, even today, we find that wherever that condition which we call modern civilisation prevails, and in proportion as it tends to prevail—wherever steam-power, electricity, or the forces of wind and water, are compelled by man's intellectual activity to act as the motor-powers in the accomplishment of human toil, wherever the delicate adaptions of scientifically constructed machinery are taking the place of the simple manipulation of the human hand—there has arisen, all the world over, a large body of males who find that their ancient fields of labour have slipped or are slipping from them, and who discover that the modern world has no place or need for them. At the gates of our dockyards, in our streets, and in our fields, are to be found everywhere, in proportion as modern civilisation is really dominant, men whose bulk and mere animal strength would have made them as warriors invaluable members of any primitive community, and who would have been valuable even in any simpler civilisation than our own, as machines of toil; but who, owing to lack of intellectual or delicate manual training, have now no form of labour to offer society which it stands really in need of, and who therefore tend to form our Great Male Unemployed—a body which finds the only powers it possesses so little needed by its fellows that, in return for its intensest physical labour, it hardly earns the poorest sustenance. The material conditions of life have been rapidly modified, and the man has not been modified with them; machinery has largely filled his place in his old field of labour, and he has found no new one.

It is from these men, men who, viewed from the broad humanitarian standpoint, are often of the most lovable and interesting type, and who might in a simpler state of society, where physical force was the dominating factor, have been the heroes, leaders, and chiefs of their people, that there arises in the modern world the bitter cry of the male unemployed: "Give us labour or we die!" (The problem of the unemployed male is, of course, not nearly so modern as that of the unemployed female. It may be said in England to have taken its rise in almost its present form as early as the fifteenth century, when economic changes began to sever the agricultural labourer from the land, and rob him of his ancient forms of social toil. Still, in its most acute form, it may be called a modern problem.)

Yet it is only upon one, and a comparatively small, section of the males of the modern civilised world that these changes in the material conditions of life have told in such fashion as to take all useful occupation from them and render them wholly or partly worthless to society. If the modern man's field of labour has contracted at one end (the physical), at the other (the intellectual) it has immeasurably expanded! If machinery and the command of inanimate motor-forces have rendered of comparatively little value the male's mere physical motor-power, the demand upon his intellectual faculties, the call for the expenditure of nervous energy, and the exercise of delicate manipulative skill in the labour of human life, have immeasurably increased.

In a million new directions forms of honoured and remunerative social labour are opening up before the feet of the modern man, which his ancestors never dreamed of; and day by day they yet increase in numbers and importance. The steamship, the hydraulic lift, the patent road-maker, the railway-train, the electric tram-car, the steam-driven mill, the Maxim gun and the torpedo boat, once made, may perform their labours with the guidance and assistance of comparatively few hands; but a whole army of men of science, engineers, clerks, and highly-trained workmen is necessary for their invention, construction, and maintenance. In the domains of art, of science, of literature, and above all in the field of politics and government, an almost infinite extension has taken place in the fields of male labour. Where in primitive times woman was often the only builder, and patterns she daubed on her hut walls or traced on her earthen vessels the only attempts at domestic art; and where later but an individual here and there was required to design a king's palace or a god's temple or to ornament it with statues or paintings, today a mighty army of men, a million strong, is employed in producing plastic art alone, both high and low, from the traceries on wall-paper and the illustrations in penny journals, to the production of the pictures and statues which adorn the national collections, and a mighty new field of toil has opened before the anciently hunting and fighting male. Where once one ancient witch-doctress may have been the only creature in a whole district who studied the nature of herbs and earths, or a solitary wizard experimenting on poisons was the only individual in a whole territory interrogating nature; and where later, a few score of alchemists and astrologers only were engaged in examining the structure of substances, or the movement of planets, today thousands of men in every civilised community are labouring to unravel the mysteries of nature, and the practical chemist, the physician, the anatomist, the engineer, the astronomer, the mathematician, the electrician, form a mighty and always increasingly important army of male labourers. Where once an isolated bard supplied a nation with its literatures, or where later a few thousand priests and men of letters wrote and transcribed for the few to read, today literature gives labour to a multitude almost as countless as a swarm of locusts. From the penny-a-liner to the artist and thinker, the demand for their labour continually increases. Where one town-crier with stout legs and lusty lungs was once all-sufficient to spread the town and country news, a score of men now sit daily pen in hand, preparing the columns of the morning's paper, and far into the night a hundred compositors are engaged in a labour which requires a higher culture of brain and finger than most ancient kings and rulers possessed. Even in the labours of war, the most brutal and primitive of the occupations lingering on into civilised life from the savage state, the new demand for labour of an intellectual kind is enormous. The invention, construction, and working of one Krupp gun, though its mere discharge hardly demands more crude muscular exertion than a savage expends in throwing his boomerang, yet represents an infinitude of intellectual care and thought, far greater than that which went to the shaping of all the weapons of a primitive army. Above all, in the domain of politics and government, where once a king or queen, aided by a handful of councillors, was alone practically concerned in the labours of national guidance or legislation; today, owing to the rapid means of intercommunication, printing, and the consequent diffusion of political and social information throughout a territory, it has become possible, for the first time, for all adults in a large community to keep themselves closely informed on all national affairs; and in every highly-civilised state the ordinary male has been almost compelled to take his share, however small, in the duties and labours of legislation and government. Thus there has opened before the mass of men a vast new sphere of labour undreamed of by their ancestors. In every direction the change which material civilisation has wrought, while it has militated against that comparatively small section of males who have nothing to offer society but the expenditure of their untrained muscular energy (inflicting much and often completely unmerited suffering upon them), has immeasurably extended the field of male labour as a whole. Never before in the history of the earth has the man's field of remunerative toil been so wide, so interesting, so complex, and in its results so all-important to society; never before has the male sex, taken as a whole, been so fully and strenuously employed.

So much is this the case, that, exactly as in the earlier conditions of society an excessive and almost crushing amount of the most important physical labour generally devolved upon the female, so under modern civilised conditions among the wealthier and fully civilised classes, an unduly excessive share of labour tends to devolve upon the male. That almost entirely modern, morbid condition, affecting brain and nervous system, and shortening the lives of thousands in modern civilised societies, which is vulgarly known as "overwork" or "nervous breakdown," is but one evidence of the even excessive share of mental toil devolving upon the modern male of the cultured classes, who, in addition to maintaining himself, has frequently dependent upon him a larger or smaller number of entirely parasitic females. But, whatever the result of the changes of modern civilisation may be with regard to the male, he certainly cannot complain that they have as a whole robbed him of his fields of labour, diminished his share in the conduct of life, or reduced him to a condition of morbid inactivity.

In our woman's field of labour, matters have tended to shape themselves wholly otherwise! The changes which have taken place during the last centuries, and which we sum up under the compendious term "modern civilisation," have tended to rob woman, not merely in part but almost wholly, of the more valuable of her ancient domain of productive and social labour; and, where there has not been a determined and conscious resistance on her part, have nowhere spontaneously tended to open out to her new and compensatory fields.

It is this fact which constitutes our modern "Woman's Labour Problem."

Our spinning-wheels are all broken; in a thousand huge buildings steam-driven looms, guided by a few hundred thousands of hands (often those of men), produce the clothings of half the world; and we dare no longer say, proudly, as of old, that we and we alone clothe our peoples.

Our hoes and our grindstones passed from us long ago, when the ploughman and the miller took our place; but for a time we kept fast possession of the kneading-trough and the brewing-vat. Today, steam often shapes our bread, and the loaves are set down at our very door—it may be by a man-driven motor-car! The history of our household drinks we know no longer; we merely see them set before us at our tables. Day by day machine-prepared and factory-produced viands take a larger and larger place in the dietary of rich and poor, till the working man's wife places before her household little that is of her own preparation; while among the wealthier classes, so far has domestic change gone that men are not unfrequently found labouring in our houses and kitchens, and even standing behind our chairs ready to do all but actually place the morsels of food between our feminine lips. The army of rosy milkmaids has passed away for ever, to give place to the cream-separator and the, largely, male-and-machinery manipulated butter pat. In every direction the ancient saw, that it was exclusively the woman's sphere to prepare the viands for her household, has become, in proportion as civilisation has perfected itself, an antiquated lie.

Even the minor domestic operations are tending to pass out of the circle of woman's labour. In modern cities our carpets are beaten, our windows cleaned, our floors polished, by machinery, or extra domestic, and often male labour. Change has gone much farther than to the mere taking from us of the preparation of the materials from which the clothing is formed. Already the domestic sewing-machine, which has supplanted almost entirely the ancient needle, begins to become antiquated, and a thousand machines driven in factories by central engines are supplying not only the husband and son, but the woman herself, with almost every article of clothing from vest to jacket; while among the wealthy classes, the male dress-designer with his hundred male-milliners and dressmakers is helping finally to explode the ancient myth, that it is woman's exclusive sphere, and a part of her domestic toil, to cut and shape the garments she or her household wear.

Year by year, day by day, there is a silently working but determined tendency for the sphere of woman's domestic labours to contract itself; and the contraction is marked exactly in proportion as that complex condition which we term "modern civilisation" is advanced.

It manifests itself more in England and America than in Italy and Spain, more in great cities than in country places, more among the wealthier classes than the poorer, and is an unfailing indication of advancing modern civilisation. (There is, indeed, often something pathetic in the attitude of many a good old mother of the race, who having survived, here and there, into the heart of our modern civilisation, is sorely puzzled by the change in woman's duties and obligations. She may be found looking into the eyes of some ancient crone, who, like herself, has survived from a previous state of civilisation, seeking there a confirmation of a view of life of which a troublous doubt has crept even into her own soul. "I," she cries, "always cured my own hams, and knitted my own socks, and made up all the linen by hand. We always did it when we were girls—but now my daughters object!" And her old crone answers her? "Yes, we did it; it's the right thing; but it's so expensive. It's so much cheaper to buy things ready made!" And they shake their heads and go their ways, feeling that the world is strangely out of joint when duty seems no more duty. Such women are, in truth, like a good old mother duck, who, having for years led her ducklings to the same pond, when that pond has been drained and nothing is left but baked mud, will still persist in bringing her younglings down to it, and walks about with flapping wings and anxious quack, trying to induce them to enter it. But the ducklings, with fresh young instincts, hear far off the delicious drippings from the new dam which has been built higher up to catch the water, and they smell the chickweed and the long grass that is growing up beside it; and absolutely refuse to disport themselves on the baked mud or to pretend to seek for worms where no worms are. And they leave the ancient mother quacking beside her pond and set out to seek for new pastures—perhaps to lose themselves upon the way?—perhaps to find them? To the old mother one is inclined to say, "Ah, good old mother duck, can you not see the world has changed? You cannot bring the water back into the dried-up pond! Mayhap it was better and pleasanter when it was there, but it has gone for ever; and, would you and yours swim again, it must be in other waters." New machinery, new duties.)

But it is not only, nor even mainly, in the sphere of women's material domestic labours that change has touched her and shrunk her ancient field of labour.

Time was, when the woman kept her children about her knees till adult years were reached. Hers was the training and influence which shaped them. From the moment when the infant first lay on her breast, till her daughters left her for marriage and her sons went to take share in man's labour,

35

they were continually under the mother's influence. Today, so complex have become even the technical and simpler branches of education, so mighty and inexorable are the demands which modern civilisation makes for specialised instruction and training for all individuals who are to survive and retain their usefulness under modern conditions, that, from the earliest years of its life, the child is of necessity largely removed from the hands of the mother, and placed in those of the specialised instructor. Among the wealthier classes, scarcely is the infant born when it passes into the hands of the trained nurse, and from hers on into the hands of the qualified teacher; till, at nine or ten, the son in certain countries often leaves his home for ever for the public school, to pass on to the college and university; while the daughter, in the hands of trained instructors and dependents, owes in the majority of cases hardly more of her education or formation to maternal toil. While even among our poorer classes, the infant school, and the public school; and later on the necessity for manual training, takes the son and often the daughter as completely, and always increasingly as civilisation advances, from the mother's control. So marked has this change in woman's ancient field of labour become, that a woman of almost any class may have borne many children and yet in early middle age be found sitting alone in an empty house, all her offspring gone from her to receive training and instruction at the hands of others. The ancient statement that the training and education of her offspring is exclusively the duty of the mother, however true it may have been with regard to a remote past, has become an absolute misstatement; and the woman who should at the present day insist on entirely educating her own offspring would, in nine cases out of ten, inflict an irreparable injury on them, because she is incompetent.

But, if possible, yet more deeply and radically have the changes of modern civilisation touched our ancient field of labour in another direction—in that very portion of the field of human labour which is peculiarly and organically ours, and which can never be wholly taken from us. Here the shrinkage has been larger than in any other direction, and touches us as women more vitally.

Time was, and still is, among almost all primitive and savage folk, when the first and all-important duty of the female to her society was to bear, to bear much, and to bear unceasingly! On her adequate and persistent performance of this passive form of labour, and of her successful feeding of her young from her own breast, and rearing it, depended, not merely the welfare, but often the very existence, of her tribe or nation. Where, as is the case among almost all barbarous peoples, the rate of infant mortality is high; where the unceasing casualties resulting from war, the chase, and acts of personal violence tend continually to reduce the number of adult males; where, surgical knowledge being still in its infancy, most wounds are fatal; where, above all, recurrent pestilence and famine, unfailing if of irregular recurrence, decimated the people, it has been all important that woman should employ her creative power to its very uttermost limits if the race were not at once to dwindle and die out. "May thy wife's womb never cease from bearing," is still today the highest expression of goodwill on the part of a native African chief to his departing guest. For, not only does the prolific woman in the primitive state contribute to the wealth and strength of her nation as a whole, but to that of her own male companion and of her family. Where the social conditions of life are so simple that, in addition to bearing and suckling the child, it is reared and nourished through childhood almost entirely through the labour and care of the mother, requiring no expenditure of tribal or family wealth on its training or education, its value as an adult enormously outweighs, both to the state and the male, the trouble and expense of rearing it, which falls almost entirely on the individual woman who bears it. The man who has twenty children to become warriors and labourers is by so much the richer and the more powerful than he who has but one; while the state whose women are prolific and labour for and rear their children stands so far insured against destruction. Incessant and persistent child-bearing is thus truly the highest duty and the most socially esteemed occupation of the primitive woman, equalling fully in social importance the labour of the man as hunter and warrior.

Even under those conditions of civilisation which have existed in the centuries which divide primitive savagery from high civilisation, the demand for continuous, unbroken child-bearing on the part of the woman as her loftiest social duty has generally been hardly less imperious. Throughout the Middle Ages of Europe, and down almost to our own day, the rate of infant mortality was almost as large as in a savage state; medical ignorance destroyed innumerable lives; antiseptic surgery being unknown, serious wounds were still almost always fatal; in the low state of sanitary science, plagues such as those which in the reign of Justinian swept across the civilised world from India to Northern Europe, well nigh depopulating the globe, or the Black Death of 1349, which in England alone swept away more than half the population of the island, were but extreme forms of the destruction of population going on continually as the result of zymotic disease; while wars were not merely far more common but, owing to the famines which almost invariably followed them, were far more destructive to human life than in our own days, and deaths by violence, whether at the hands of the state or as the result of personal enmity, were of daily occurrence in all lands. Under these conditions abstinence on the part of woman from incessant child-bearing might have led to almost the same serious diminution or even extinction of her people, as in the savage state; while the very existence of her civilisation depended on the production of an immense number of individuals as beasts of burden, without the expenditure of whose crude muscular force in physical labour of agriculture and manufacture those intermediate civilisations would, in the absence of machinery, have been impossible. Twenty men had to be born, fed at the breast, and reared by women to perform the crude brute labour which is performed today by one small, well-adjusted steam crane; and the demand for large masses of human creatures as mere reservoirs of motor force for accomplishing the simplest processes was imperative. So strong, indeed, was the consciousness of the importance to society of continuous child-bearing on the part of woman, that as late as the middle of the sixteenth century Martin Luther wrote: "If a woman becomes weary or at last dead from bearing, that matters not; let her only die from bearing, she is there to do it;" and he doubtless gave expression, in a crude and somewhat brutal form, to a conviction common to the bulk of his contemporaries, both male and female.

Today, this condition has almost completely reversed itself.

The advance of science and the amelioration of the physical conditions of life tend rapidly toward a diminution of human mortality. The infant death-rate among the upper classes in modern civilisations has fallen by more than one-half; while among poorer classes it is already, though slowly, falling: the increased knowledge of the laws of sanitation has made among all highly civilised peoples the depopulation by plague a thing of the past, and the discoveries of the next twenty or thirty years will probably do away for ever with the danger to man of zymotic disease. Famines of the old desolating type have become an impossibility where rapid means of transportation convey the superfluity of one land to supply the lack of another; and war and deeds of violence, though still lingering among us, have already become episodal in the lives of nations as of individuals; while the vast advances in antiseptic surgery have caused even the effects of wounds and dismemberments to become only very partially fatal to human life. All these changes have tended to diminish human mortality and protract human life; and they have today already made it possible for a race not only to maintain its numbers, but even to increase them, with a comparatively small expenditure of woman's vitality in the passive labour of child-bearing.

But yet more seriously has the demand for woman's labour as child-bearer been diminished by change in another direction.

Every mechanical invention which lessens the necessity for rough, untrained, muscular, human labour, diminishes also the social demand upon woman as the producer in large masses of such labourers. Already throughout the modern civilised world we have reached a point at which the social demand is not merely for human creatures in the bulk for use as beasts of burden, but, rather, and only, for such human creatures as shall be so trained and cultured as to be fitted for the performance of the more complex duties of modern life. Not, now, merely for many men, but, rather, for few men, and those few, well born and well instructed, is the modern demand. And the woman who today merely produces twelve children and suckles them, and then turns them loose on her society and family, is regarded, and rightly so, as a curse and down draught, and not the productive labourer, of her community. Indeed, so difficult and expensive has become in the modern world the rearing and training of even one individual, in a manner suited to fit it for coping with the complexities and difficulties of civilised life, that, to the family as well as to the state, unlimited fecundity on the part of the female has already, in most cases, become irremediable evil; whether it be in the case of the artisan, who at the cost of immense self-sacrifice must support and train his children till their twelfth or fourteenth year, if they are ever to become even skilled manual labourers, and who if his family be large often sinks beneath the burden, allowing his offspring, untaught and untrained, to become waste products of human life; or, in that of the professional man, who by his mental toil is compelled to support and educate, at immense expense, his sons till they are twenty or older, and to sustain his daughters, often throughout their whole lives should they not marry, and to whom a large family proves often no less disastrous; while the state whose women produce recklessly large masses of individuals in excess of those for whom they can provide instruction and nourishment is a state, in so far, tending toward deterioration. The commandment to the modern woman is now not simply "Thou shalt bear," but rather, "Thou shalt not bear in excess of thy power to rear and train satisfactorily;" and the woman who should today appear at the door of a workhouse or the tribunal of the poor-law guardians followed by her twelve infants, demanding honourable sustenance for them and herself in return for the labour she had undergone in producing them, would meet with but short shrift. And the modern man who on his wedding-day should be greeted with the ancient good wish, that he might become the father of twenty sons and twenty daughters, would regard it as a malediction rather than a blessing. It is certain that the time is now rapidly approaching when child-bearing will be regarded rather as a lofty privilege, permissible only to those who have shown their power rightly to train and provide for their offspring, than a labour which in itself, and under whatever conditions performed, is beneficial to society. (The difference between the primitive and modern view on this matter is aptly and quaintly illustrated by two incidents. Seeing a certain Bantu woman who appeared better cared for, less hard worked, and happier than the mass of her companions, we made inquiry, and found that she had two impotent brothers; because of this she herself had not married, but had borne by different men fourteen children, all of whom when grown she had given to her brothers. "They are fond of me because I have given them so many children, therefore I have not to work like the other women; and my brothers give me plenty of mealies and milk," she replied, complacently, when questioned, "and our family will not die out." And this person, whose conduct was so emphatically anti-social on all sides when viewed from the modern standpoint, was evidently regarded as pre-eminently of value to her family and to society because of her mere fecundity. On the other hand, a few weeks back appeared an account in the London papers of an individual who, taken up at the East End for some brutal offence, blubbered out in court that she was the mother of twenty children. "You should be ashamed of yourself!" responded the magistrate; "a woman capable of such conduct would be capable of doing anything!" and the fine was remorselessly inflicted. Undoubtedly, if somewhat brutally, the magistrate yet gave true voice to the modern view on the subject of excessive and reckless child-bearing.)

Further, owing partly to the diminished demand for child-bearing, rising from the extreme difficulty and expense of rearing and education, and to many other complex social causes, to which we shall return later, millions of women in our modern societies are so placed as to be absolutely compelled to go through life not merely childless, but without sex relationship in any form whatever; while another mighty army of women is reduced by the dislocations of our civilisation to accepting sexual relationships which practically negate child-bearing, and whose only product is physical and moral disease.

Thus, it has come to pass that vast numbers of us are, by modern social conditions, prohibited from child-bearing at all; and that even those among us who are child-bearers are required, in proportion as the class of race to which we belong stands high in the scale of civilisation, to produce in most cases a limited number of offspring; so that even for these of us, child-bearing and suckling, instead of filling the entire circle of female life from the first appearance of puberty to the end of middle age, becomes an episodal occupation, employing from three or four to ten or twenty of the threescore-and-ten-years which are allotted to human life. In such societies the statement (so profoundly true when made with regard to most savage societies, and even largely true with regard to those in the intermediate stages of civilisation) that the main and continuous occupation of all women from puberty to age is the bearing and suckling of children, and that this occupation must fully satisfy all her needs for social labour and activity, becomes an antiquated and unmitigated misstatement.

Not only are millions of our women precluded from ever

bearing a child, but for those of us who do bear the demand is ever increasingly in civilised societies coupled with the condition that if we would act socially we must restrict our powers. (As regards modern civilised nations, we find that those whose birthrate is the highest per woman are by no means the happiest, most enlightened, or powerful; nor do we even find that the population always increases in proportion to the births. France, which in many respects leads in the van of civilisation, has one of the lowest birthrates per woman in Europe; and among the free and enlightened population of Switzerland and Scandinavia the birthrate is often exceedingly low; while Ireland, one of the most unhappy and weak of European nations, had long one of the highest birthrates, without any proportional increase in population or power. With regard to the different classes in one community, the same effect is observable. The birthrate per woman is higher among the lowest and most ignorant classes in the back slums of our great cities, than among the women of the upper and cultured classes, mainly because the age at which marriages are contracted always tends to become higher as the culture and intelligence of individuals rises, but also because of the regulation of the number of births after marriage. Yet the number of children reared to adult years among the more intelligent classes probably equals or exceeds those of the lowest, owing to the high rate of infant mortality where births are excessive.)

Looking round, then, with the uttermost impartiality we can command, on the entire field of woman's ancient and traditional labours, we find that fully three-fourths of it have shrunk away for ever, and that the remaining fourth still tends to shrink.

It is this great fact, so often and so completely overlooked, which lies as the propelling force behind that vast and restless "Woman's Movement" which marks our day. It is this fact, whether clearly and intellectually grasped, or, as is more often the case, vaguely and painfully felt, which awakes in the hearts of the ablest modern European women their passionate, and at times it would seem almost incoherent, cry for new forms of labour and new fields for the exercise of their powers.

Thrown into strict logical form, our demand is this: We do not ask that the wheels of time should reverse themselves, or the stream of life flow backward. We do not ask that our ancient spinning-wheels be again resuscitated and placed in our hands; we do not demand that our old grindstones and hoes be returned to us, or that man should again betake himself entirely to his ancient province of war and the chase, leaving to us all domestic and civil labour. We do not even demand that society shall immediately so reconstruct itself that every woman may be again a child-bearer (deep and over-mastering as lies the hunger for motherhood in every virile woman's heart!); neither do we demand that the children whom we bear shall again be put exclusively into our hands to train. This, we know, cannot be. The past material conditions of life have gone for ever; no will of man can recall them; but this is our demand: We demand that, in that strange new world that is arising alike upon the man and the woman, where nothing is as it was, and all things are assuming new shapes and relations, that in this new world we also shall have our share of honoured and socially useful human toil, our full half of the labour of the Children of Woman. We demand nothing more than this, and we will take nothing less. This is our "WOMAN'S RIGHT!"

CHAPTER II

PARASITISM
(*Continued*)

Is it to be, that, in the future, machinery and the captive motor-forces of nature are largely to take the place of human hand and foot in the labour of clothing and feeding the nations; are these branches of industry to be no longer domestic labours?—then, we demand in the factory, the warehouse, and the field, wherever machinery has usurped our ancient labour-ground, that we also should have our place, as guiders, controllers, and possessors. Is child-bearing to become the labour of but a portion of our sex?—then we demand for those among us who are allowed to take no share in it, compensatory and equally honourable and important fields of social toil. Is the training of human creatures to become a yet more and more onerous and laborious occupation, their education and culture to become increasingly a high art, complex and scientific?—if so, then, we demand that high and complex culture and training which shall fit us for instructing the race which we bring into the world. Is the demand for child-bearing to become so diminished that, even in the lives of those among us who are child-bearers, it shall fill no more than half a dozen years out of the three-score-and-ten of human life?—then we demand that an additional outlet be ours which shall fill up with dignity and value the tale of the years not so employed. Is intellectual labour to take ever and increasingly the place of crude muscular exertion in the labour of life?—then we demand for ourselves that culture and the freedom of action which alone can yield us the knowledge of life and the intellectual vigour and strength which will enable us to undertake the same share of mental which we have borne in the past in physical labours of life. Are the rulers of the race to be no more its kings and queens, but the mass of the peoples?— then we, one-half of the nations, demand our full queens' share in the duties and labours of government and legislation. Slowly but determinately, as the old fields of labour close up and are submerged behind us, we demand entrance into the new.

We make this demand, not for our own sakes alone, but for the succour of the race.

A horseman, riding along on a dark night in an unknown land, may chance to feel his horse start beneath him; rearing, it may almost hurl him to the earth: in the darkness he may curse his beast, and believe its aim is simply to cast him off, and free itself for ever of its burden. But when the morning dawns and lights the hills and valleys he has travelled, looking backward, he may perceive that the spot where his beast reared, planting its feet into the earth, and where it refused to move farther on the old road, was indeed the edge of a mighty precipice, down which one step more would have precipitated both horse and rider. And he may then see that it was an instinct wiser than his own which lead his creature, though in the dark, to leap backward, seeking a new path along which both might travel. (Is it not recorded that even Balaam's ass on which he rode saw the angel with flaming sword, but Balaam saw it not?)

In the confusion and darkness of the present, it may well seem to some, that woman, in her desire to seek for new paths of labour and employment, is guided only by an irresponsible impulse; or that she seeks selfishly only her own good, at the cost of that of the race, which she has so long and faithfully borne onward. But, when a clearer future shall have arisen and the obscuring mists of the present have been dissipated, may it not then be clearly manifest that not for herself alone, but for her entire race, has woman sought her new paths?

For let it be noted exactly what our position is, who today, as women, are demanding new fields of labour and a reconstruction of our relationship with life.

It is often said that the labour problem before the modern woman and that before the unemployed or partially or almost uselessly employed male, are absolutely identical; and that therefore, when the male labour problem of our age solves itself, that of the woman will of necessity have met its solution also.

This statement, with a certain specious semblance of truth, is yet, we believe, radically and fundamentally false. It is true that both the male and the female problems of our age have taken their rise largely in the same rapid material changes which during the last centuries, and more especially the last ninety years, have altered the face of the human world. Both men and women have been robbed by those changes of their ancient remunerative fields of social work: here the resemblance stops. The male, from whom the changes of modern civilisation have taken his ancient field of labour, has but one choice before him: he must find new fields of labour, or he must perish. Society will not ultimately support him in an absolutely quiescent and almost useless condition. If he does not vigorously exert himself in some direction or other (the direction may even be predatory) he must ultimately be annihilated. Individual drones, both among the wealthiest and the poorest classes (millionaires' sons, dukes, or tramps), may in isolated cases be preserved, and allowed to reproduce themselves without any exertion or activity of mind or body, but a vast body of males who, having lost their old forms of social employment, should refuse in any way to exert themselves or seek for new, would at no great length of time become extinct. There never has been, and as far as can be seen, there never will be, a time when the majority of the males in any society will be supported by the rest of the males in a condition of perfect mental and physical inactivity. "Find labour or die," is the choice ultimately put before the human male today, as in the past; and this constitutes his labour problem. (The nearest approach to complete parasitism on the part of a vast body of males occurred, perhaps, in ancient Rome at the time of the decay and downfall of the Empire, when the bulk of the population, male as well as female, was fed on imported corn, wine, and oil, and supplied even with entertainment, almost entirely without exertion or labour of any kind; but this condition was of short duration, and speedily contributed to the downfall of the diseased Empire itself. Among the wealthy and so-called upper classes, the males of various aristocracies have frequently tended to become completely parasitic after a lapse of time, but such a condition has always been met by a short and sharp remedy; and the class has fallen, or become extinct. The condition of the males of the upper classes in France before the Revolution affords an interesting illustration of this point.)

The labour of the man may not always be useful in the highest sense to his society, or it may even be distinctly harmful and antisocial, as in the case of the robber-barons of the Middle Ages, who lived by capturing and despoiling all who passed by their castles; or as in the case of the share speculators, stock-jobbers, ring-and-corner capitalists, and monopolists of the present day, who feed upon the productive labours of society without contributing anything to its welfare. But even males so occupied are compelled to expend a vast amount of energy and even a low intelligence in their callings; and, however injurious to their societies, they run no personal risk of handing down effete and enervated constitutions to their race. Whether beneficially or unbeneficially, the human male must, generally speaking, employ his intellect, or his muscle, or die.

The position of the unemployed modern female is one wholly different. The choice before her, as her ancient fields of domestic labour slip from her, is not generally or often at the present day the choice between finding new fields of labour, or death; but one far more serious in its ultimate reaction on humanity as a whole—it is the choice between finding new forms of labour or sinking slowly into a condition of more or less complete and passive sex-parasitism! (It is not without profound interest to note the varying phenomena of sex-parasitism as they present themselves in the animal world, both in the male and in the female form. Though among the greater number of species in the animal world the female form is larger and more powerful rather than the male (e.g., among birds of prey, such as eagles, falcons, vultures, &c., and among fishes, insects, &c.), yet sex-parasitism appears among both sex forms. In certain sea-creatures, for example, the female carries about in the folds of her covering three or four minute and quite inactive males, who are entirely passive and dependent upon her. Among termites, on the other hand, the female has so far degenerated that she has entirely lost the power of locomotion; she can no longer provide herself or her offspring with nourishment, or defend or even clean herself; she has become a mere passive, distended bag of eggs, without intelligence or activity, she and her offspring existing through the exertions of the workers of the community. Among other insects, such, for example, as certain ticks, another form of female parasitism prevails, and while the male remains a complex, highly active, and winded creature, the female, fastening herself by the head into the flesh of some living animal and sucking its blood, has lost wings and all activity, and power of locomotion; having become a mere distended bladder, which when filled with eggs bursts and ends a parasitic existence which has hardly been life. It is not impossible, and it appears, indeed, highly probable, that it has been this degeneration and parasitism on the part of the female which has set its limitation to the evolution of ants, creatures which, having reached a point of mental development in some respects almost as high as that of man, have yet become curiously and immovably arrested. The whole question of sex-parasitism among the lower animals is one throwing suggestive and instructive side-lights on human social problems, but is too extensive to be here entered on.)

Again and again in the history of the past, when among human creatures a certain stage of material civilisation has been reached, a curious tendency has manifested itself for the human female to become more or less parasitic; social conditions tend to rob her of all forms of active, conscious, social labour, and to reduce her, like the field-tick, to the passive exercise of her sex functions alone. And the result of this parasitism has invariably been the decay in vitality and intelligence of the female, followed after a longer or shorter period by that of her male descendants and her entire society.

Nevertheless, in the history of the past the dangers of the sex-parasitism have never threatened more than a small section of the females of the human race, those exclusively of some comparatively small dominant race or class; the mass of women beneath them being still compelled to assume many forms of strenuous activity. It is at the present day, and under the peculiar conditions of our modern civilisation, that for the first time sex-parasitism has become a danger, more or less remote, to the mass of civilised women, perhaps ultimately to all.

In the very early stages of human growth, the sexual parasitism and degeneration of the female formed no possible source of social danger. Where the conditions of life rendered it inevitable that all the labour of a community should be performed by the members of that community for themselves, without the assistance of slaves or machinery, the tendency has always been rather to throw an excessive amount of social labour on the female. Under no conditions, at no time, in no place, in the history of the world have the males of any period, of any nation, or of any class, shown the slightest inclination to allow their own females to become inactive or parasitic, so long as the actual muscular labour of feeding and clothing them would in that case have devolved upon themselves!

The parasitism of the human female becomes a possibility only when a point in civilisation is reached (such as that which was attained in the ancient civilisations of Greece, Rome, Persia, Assyria, India, and such as today exists in many of the civilisations of the East, such as those of China and Turkey), when, owing to the extensive employment of the labour of slaves, or of subject races or classes, the dominant race or class has become so liberally supplied with the material goods of life, that mere physical toil on the part of its own female members has become unnecessary. It is when this point has been reached, and never before, that the symptoms of female parasitism have in the past almost invariably tended to manifest themselves, and have become a social danger. The males of the dominant class have almost always contrived to absorb to themselves the new intellectual occupations, with the absence of necessity for the old forms of physical toil made possible in their societies; and the females of the dominant class or race, for whose muscular labours there was now also no longer any need, not succeeding in grasping or attaining to these new forms of labour, have sunk into a state in which, performing no species of active social duty, they have existed through the passive performance of sexual functions alone, with how much or how little of discontent will now never be known, since no literary record has been made by the woman of the past, of her desires or sorrows. Then, in place of the active labouring woman, upholding society by her toil, has come the effete wife, concubine, or prostitute, clad in fine raiment, the work of others' fingers; fed on luxurious viands, the result of others' toil, waited on and tended by the labour of others. The need for her physical labour having gone, and mental industry not having taken its place, she bedecked and scented her person, or had it bedecked and scented for her, she lay upon her sofa, or drove or was carried out in her vehicle, and, loaded with jewels, she sought by dissipations and amusements to fill up the inordinate blank left by the lack of productive activity. And as the hand whitened and frame softened, till, at last, the very duties of motherhood, which were all the constitution of her life left her, became distasteful, and, from the instant when her infant came damp from her womb, it passed into the hands of others, to be tended and reared by them; and from youth to age her offspring often owed nothing to her personal toil. In many cases so complete was her enervation, that at last the very joy of giving life, the glory and beatitude of a virile womanhood, became distasteful; and she sought to evade it, not because of its interference with more imperious duties to those already born of her, or to her society, but because her existence of inactivity had robbed her of all joy in strenuous exertion and endurance in any form. Finely clad, tenderly housed, life became for her merely the gratification of her own physical and sexual appetites, and the appetites of the male, through the stimulation of which she could maintain herself. And, whether as kept wife, kept mistress, or prostitute, she contributed nothing to the active and sustaining labours of her society. She had attained to the full development of that type which, whether in modern Paris or New York or London, or in ancient Greece, Assyria, or Rome, is essentially one in its features, its nature, and its results. She was the "fine lady," the human female parasite—the most deadly microbe which can make its appearance on the surface of any social organism. (The relation of female parasitism generally, to the peculiar phenomenon of prostitution, is fundamental. Prostitution can never be adequately dealt with, either from the moral or the scientific standpoint, unless its relation to the general phenomenon of female parasitism be fully recognised. It is the failure to do this which leaves so painful a sense of abortion on the mind, after listening to most modern utterances on the question, whether made from the emotional platform of the moral reformer, or the intellectual platform of the would-be scientist. We are left with a feeling that the matter has been handled but not dealt with: that the knife has not reached the core.)

Wherever in the history of the past this type has reached its full development and has comprised the bulk of the females belonging to any dominant class or race, it has heralded its decay. In Assyria, Greece, Rome, Persia, as in Turkey today, the same material conditions have produced the same social disease among wealthy and dominant races; and again and again when the nation so affected has come into contact with nations more healthily constituted, this diseased condition has contributed to its destruction.

In ancient Greece, in its superb and virile youth, its womanhood was richly and even heavily endowed with duties and occupations. Not the mass of the woman alone, but the king's wife and the prince's daughter do we find going to the well to bear water, cleansing the household linen in the streams, feeding and doctoring their households, manufacturing the clothing of their race, and performing even a share of the highest social functions as priestesses and prophetesses. It was from the bodies of such women as these that sprang that race of heroes, thinkers, and artists who laid the foundations of Grecian greatness. These females underlay their society as the solid and deeply buried foundations underlay the more visible and ornate portions of a great temple, making its structure and persistence possible. In Greece, after a certain lapse of time, these virile labouring women in the upper classes were to be found no more. The accumulated wealth of the dominant race, gathered through the labour of slaves and subject people, had so immensely increased that there was no longer a call for physical labour on the part of the dominant womanhood; immured within the walls of their houses as wives or mistresses, waited on by slaves and dependents, they no longer sustained by their exertion either their own life or the life of their people. The males absorbed the intellectual labours of life; slaves and dependents the physical. For a moment, at the end of the fifth and beginning of the fourth century, when the womanhood of Greece had already internally decayed, there was indeed a brilliant intellectual efflorescence among her males, like to the gorgeous colours in the sunset sky when the sun is already sinking; but the heart of Greece was already rotting and her vigour failing. Increasingly, division and dissimilarity arose between male and female, as the male advanced in culture and entered upon new fields of intellectual toil while the female sank passively backward and lower in the scale of life, and thus was made ultimately a chasm which even sexual love could not bridge. The abnormal institution of avowed inter-male sexual relations upon the highest plane was one, and the most serious result, of this severance. The inevitable and invincible desire of all highly developed human natures, to blend with their sexual relationships their highest intellectual interests and sympathies, could find no satisfaction or response in the relationship between the immured, comparatively ignorant and helpless females of the upper classes, in Greece, and the brilliant, cultured, and many-sided males who formed its dominant class in the fifth and fourth centuries. Man turned towards man; and parenthood, the divine gift of imparting human life, was severed from the loftiest and profoundest phases of human emotion: Xanthippe fretted out her ignorant and miserable little life between the walls of her house, and Socrates lay in the Agora, discussing philosophy and morals with Alcibiades; and the race decayed at its core. (See Jowett's translation of Plato's "Banquet"; but for full light on this important question the entire literature of Greece in the fifth and fourth centuries B.C. should be studied.) Here and there an Aspasia, or earlier still a Sappho, burst through the confining bonds of woman's environment, and with the force of irresistible genius broke triumphantly into new fields of action and powerful mental activity, standing side by side with the male; but their cases were exceptional. Had they, or such as they, been able to tread down a pathway, along which the mass of Grecian women might have followed them; had it been possible for the bulk of the women of the dominant race in Greece at the end of the fifth century to rise from their condition of supine inaction and ignorance and to have taken their share in the intellectual labours and stern activities of their race, Greece would never have fallen, as she fell at the end of the fourth century, instantaneously and completely, as a rotten puff-ball falls in at the touch of a healthy finger; first, before the briberies of Philip, and then yet more completely before the arms of his yet more warlike son, who was also the son of the fierce, virile, and indomitable Olympia. (Like almost all men remarkable for either good or evil, Alexander inherited from his mother his most notable qualities—his courage, his intellectual activity, and an ambition indifferent to any means that made for his own end. Fearless in her life, she fearlessly met death "with a courage worthy of her rank and domineering character, when her hour of retribution came"; and Alexander is incomprehensible till we recognise him as rising from the womb of Olympia.) Nor could she have been swept clean, a few hundred years later, from Thessaly to Sparta, from Corinth to Ephesus, her temples destroyed, her effete women captured by the hordes of the Goths—a people less skilfully armed and less civilised than the descendants of the race of Pericles and Leonidas, but who were a branch of that great Teutonic folk whose monogamous domestic life was sound at the core, and whose fearless, labouring, and resolute women yet bore for the men they followed to the ends of the earth, what Spartan women once said they alone bore—men.

In Rome, in the days of her virtue and vigour, the Roman matron laboured mightily, and bore on her shoulders her full half of the social burden, though her sphere of labour and influence was even somewhat smaller than that of the Teutonic sisterhood whose descendants were finally to supplant her own. From the vestal virgin to the matron, the Roman woman in the days of the nation's health and growth fulfilled lofty functions and bore the whole weight of domestic toil. From the days of Lucretia, the great Roman dame whom we find spinning with her handmaidens deep into the night, and whose personal dignity was so dear to her that, violated, she sought only death, to those of the mother of the Gracchi, one of the last of the great line, we find everywhere, erect, labouring, and resolute, the Roman woman who gave birth to the men who built up Roman greatness. A few centuries later, and Rome also had reached that dangerous spot in the order of social change which Greece had reached centuries before her. Slave labour and the enjoyment of the unlimited spoils of subject races had done away for ever with the demand for physical labour on the part of the members of the dominant race. Then came the period when the male still occupied himself with the duties of war and government, of legislation and self-culture; but the Roman matron had already ceased for ever from her toils. Decked in jewels and fine clothing, brought at the cost of infinite human labour from the ends of the earth, nourished on delicate victuals, prepared by others' hands, she sought now only with amusement to pass away a life that no longer offered her the excitement and joy of active productive exertion. She frequented theatres or baths, or reclined on her sofa, or drove in her chariot; and like more modern counterparts, painted herself, wore patches, affected an artistic walk, and a handshake with the elbow raised and the fingers hanging down. Her children were reared by dependents; and in the intellectual labour and government of her age she took small part, and was fit to take none. There were not wanting writers and thinkers who saw clearly the end to which the enervation of the female was tending, and who were not sparing in their denunciations. "Time was," cries one Roman writer of that age, "when the matron turned the spindle with the hand and kept at the same time the pot in her eye that the pottage might not be singed, but now," he adds bitterly, "when the wife, loaded with jewels, reposes among pillows, or seeks the dissipation of baths and theatres, all things go downward and the state decays." Yet neither he nor that large body of writers and thinkers who saw the condition towards which the parasitism of woman was tending to reduce society, preached any adequate remedy. (Indeed, must not the protest and the remedy in all such cases, if they are to be of any avail, take their rise within the diseased class itself?)

Thoughtful men sighed over the present and yearned for the past, nor seem to have perceived that it was irrevocably gone; that the Roman lady who, with a hundred servants standing idle about her, should, in imitation of her ancestress, have gone out with her pitcher on her head to draw water from the well, while in all her own courtyards pipe-led streams gushed forth, would have acted the part of the pretender; that had she insisted on resuscitating her loom and had sat up all night to spin, she could never have produced those fabrics which alone her household demanded, and would have been but a puerile actor; that it was not by attempting to return to the ancient and for ever closed fields of toil, but by entering upon new, that she could alone serve her race and retain her own dignity and virility. That not by bearing water and weaving linen, but by so training and disciplining herself that she should be fitted to bear her share in the labour necessary to the just and wise guidance of a great empire, and be capable of training a race of men adequate to exercise an enlightened, merciful, and beneficent rule over the vast masses of subject people—that so, and so only, could she fulfil her duty toward the new society about her, and bear its burden together with man, as her ancestresses of bygone generations had borne the burden of theirs.

That in this direction, and this alone, lay the only possible remedy for the evils of woman's condition, was a conception apparently grasped by none; and the female sank lower and lower, till the image of the parasitic woman of Rome (with a rag of the old Roman intensity left even in her degradation!)— seeking madly by pursuit of pleasure and sensuality to fill the void left by the lack of honourable activity; accepting lust in the place of love, ease in the place of exertion, and an unlimited consumption in the place of production; too enervated at last to care even to produce offspring, and shrinking from every form of endurance—remains, even to the present day, the most perfect, and therefore the most appalling, picture of the parasite female that earth has produced—a picture only less terrible than it is pathetic.

We recognise that it was inevitable that this womanhood— born it would seem from its elevation to guide and enlighten a world, and in place thereof feeding on it—should at last have given birth to a manhood as effete as itself, and that both should in the end have been swept away before the march of those Teutonic folk, whose women were virile and could give birth to men; a folk among whom the woman received on the morning of her marriage, from the man who was to be her companion through life, no contemptible trinket to hang about her throat or limbs, but a shield, a spear, a sword, and a yoke of oxen, while she bestowed on him in return a suit of armour, in token that they two were henceforth to be one in toil and in the facing of danger; that she too should dare with him in war and suffer with him in peace; and of whom another writer tells us, that their women not only bore the race and fed it at their breasts without the help of others' hands, but that they undertook the whole management of house and lands, leaving the males free for war and chase; of whom Suetonius tells us, that when Augustus Caesar demanded hostages from a tribe, he took women, not men, because he found by experience that the women were more regarded than men, and of whom Strabo says, that so highly did the Germanic races value the intellect of their women that they regarded them as inspired, and entered into no war or great undertaking without their advice and counsel; while among the Cimbrian women who accompanied their husbands in the invasion of Italy were certain who marched barefooted in the midst of the lines, distinguished by their white hair and milk-white robes, and who were regarded as inspired, and of whom Florus, describing an early Roman victory, says, "The conflict was not less fierce and obstinate with the wives of the vanquished; in their carts and wagons they formed a line of battle, and from their elevated situation, as from so many turrets, annoyed the Romans with their poles and lances. (The South African Boer woman after two thousand years appears not wholly to have forgotten the ancestral tactics.) Their death was as glorious as their martial spirit. Finding that all was lost, they strangled their children, and either destroyed themselves in one scene of mutual slaughter, or with the sashes that bound up their hair suspended themselves by the neck to the boughs of trees or the tops of their wagons." It is of these women that Valerius Maximus says, that, "If the gods on the day of battle had inspired the men with equal fortitude, Marius would never have boasted of his Teutonic victory;" and of whom Tacitus, speaking of those women who accompanied their husbands to war, remarks, "These are the darling witnesses of his conduct, the applauders of his valour, at once beloved and valued. The wounded seek their mothers and their wives; undismayed at the sight, the women count each honourable scar and suck the gushing blood. They are even hardy enough to mix with the combatants, administering refreshment and exhorting them to deeds of valour," and adds moreover, that "To be contented with one wife was peculiar to the Germans; while the woman was contented with one husband, as with one life, one mind, one body."

It was inevitable that before the sons of women such as these, the sons of the parasitic Roman should be swept from existence, as the offspring of the caged canary would fall in conflict with the offspring of the free.

Again and again with wearisome reiteration, the same story repeats itself. Among the Jews in the days of their health and growth, we find their women bearing the major weight of agricultural and domestic toil, full always of labour and care— from Rachel, whom Jacob met and loved as she watered her father's flocks, to Ruth, the ancestress of a line of kings and heroes, whom her Boas noted labouring in the harvest-fields; from Sarah, kneading and baking cakes for Abraham's prophetic visitors, to Miriam, prophetess and singer, and Deborah, who judging Israel from beneath her palm-tree, "and the land had rest for forty years." Everywhere the ancient Jewish woman appears, an active sustaining power among her people; and perhaps the noblest picture of the labouring woman to be found in any literature is contained in the Jewish writings, indited possibly at the very time when the labouring woman was for the first time tending among a section of the Jews to become a thing of the past; when already Solomon, with his seven hundred parasitic

59

wives and three hundred parasitic concubines, loomed large on the horizon of the national life, to take the place of flock-tending Rachel and gleaning Ruth, and to produce amid their palaces of cedar and gold, among them all, no Joseph or David, but in the way of descendant only a Rehoboam, under whose hand the kingdom was to totter to its fall. (The picture of the labouring as opposed to the parasitic ideal of womanhood appears under the heading, "The words of King Lemuel; the oracle which his mother taught him.") At risk of presenting the reader with that with which he is already painfully familiar, we here transcribe the passage; which, allowing for differences in material and intellectual surroundings, paints also the ideal of the labouring womanhood of the present and of the future:—

> "Her price is far above rubies,
> The heart of her husband trusteth in her,
> And he shall have no lack of gain,
> She doeth him good and not evil
> All the days of her life,
> She seeketh wool and flax,
> And worketh willingly with her hands,
> She is like the merchant ships;
> She bringeth her food, from afar,
> She riseth up while it is yet night
> And giveth meat to her household,
> And their task to her maidens,
> She considereth a field, and buyeth it;
> With the fruit of her hands she planteth a vineyard.
> She girdeth her loins with strength,
> And maketh strong her arms.
> She perceiveth that her merchandise is profitable;
> Her lamp goeth not out by night,
> She layeth her hands to the distaff,
> And her hands hold the spindle.
> She spreadeth out her hand to the poor:

Yea, she reacheth forth her hands to the needy,
She is not afraid of the snow for her household,
For all her household are clothed with scarlet.
She maketh herself carpets of tapestry;
Her clothing is fine and purple.
Her husband is known in the gates,
When he sitteth among the elders of the land,
She maketh linen garments and selleth them,
And delivereth girdles unto the merchant.
Strength and dignity are her clothing;
And she laugheth at the time to come.
She openeth her mouth with wisdom,
And the law of kindness is on her tongue,
She looketh well to the ways of her household,
And eateth not the bread of idleness.
Her children rise up and call her blessed,
Her husband also, and he praiseth her, saying,
Many daughters have done virtuously,
But thou excellest them all,
Give her the fruit of her hand,
And let her works praise her in the gate."

In the East today the same story has wearisomely written itself: in China, where the present vitality and power of the most ancient of existing civilisations may be measured accurately by the length of its woman's shoes; in Turkish harems, where one of the noblest dominant Aryan races the world has yet produced, is being slowly suffocated in the arms of a parasite womanhood, and might, indeed, along ago have been obliterated, had not a certain virility and strength been continually reinfused into it through the persons of purchased wives, who in early childhood and youth had been themselves active labouring peasants. Everywhere, in the past as in the present, the parasitism of the female heralds the decay of a nation or class, and as invariably indicates disease as the pustules of smallpox upon the skin indicate the existence of a purulent virus in the system.

We are, indeed, far from asserting that the civilisations of the past which have decayed, have decayed alone through the parasitism of their females. Vast, far-reaching social phenomena have invariably causes and reactions immeasurably too complex to be summed up under one so simple a term. Behind the phenomenon of female parasitism has always lain another and yet larger social phenomenon; it has invariably been preceded, as we have seen, by the subjugation of large bodies of other human creatures, either as slaves, subject races, or classes; and as the result of the excessive labours of those classes there has always been an accumulation of unearned wealth in the hands of the dominant class or race. It has invariably been by feeding on this wealth, the result of forced or ill-paid labour, that the female of the dominant race or class has in the past lost her activity and has come to exist purely through the passive performance of her sexual functions. Without slaves or subject classes to perform the crude physical labours of life and produce superfluous wealth, the parasitism of the female would, in the past, have been an impossibility.

There is, therefore, a profound truth in that universal saw which states that the decay of the great nations and civilisations of the past has resulted from the enervation caused by excessive wealth and luxury; and there is a further, and if possible more profound, truth underlying the statement that their destruction has ultimately been the result of the enervation of the entire race, male and female.

But when we come further to inquire how, exactly, this process of decay took place, we shall find that the part which the parasitism of the female has played has been fundamental. The mere use of any of the material products of labour, which we term wealth, can never in itself produce that decay, physical or mental, which precedes the downfall of great civilised nations. The eating of salmon at ten shillings a pound can in itself no more debilitate and corrupt the moral, intellectual, and physical constitution of the man consuming it, than it could enervate his naked forefathers who speared it in their rivers for food; the fact that an individual wears a robe made from the filaments of a worm, can no more deteriorate his spiritual or physical fibre, than were it made of sheep's wool; an entire race, housed in marble palaces, faring delicately, and clad in silks, and surrounded by the noblest products of literature and plastic art, so those palaces, viands, garments, and products of art were the result of their own labours, could never be enervated by them. The debilitating effect of wealth sets in at that point exactly (and never before) at which the supply of material necessaries and comforts, and of aesthetic enjoyments, clogs the individuality, causing it to rest satisfied in the mere passive possession of the results of the labour of others, without feeling any necessity or desire for further productive activity of its own. (Of the other deleterious effects of unearned wealth on the individual or class possessing it, such as its power of lessening human sympathy, &c., &c., we do not now speak, as while ultimately and indirectly, undoubtedly, tending to disintegrate a society, they do not necessarily and immediately enervate it, which enervation is the point we are here considering.)

The exact material condition at which this point will be reached will vary, not only with the race and the age, but with the individual. A Marcus Aurelius in a palace of gold and marble was able to retain his simplicity and virility as completely as though he had lived in a cow-herd's hut; while on the other hand, it is quite possible for the wife of a savage chief who has but four slaves to bring her her corn and milk and spread her skins in the sun, to become almost as purely parasitic as the most delicately pampered female of fashion in ancient Rome, or modern Paris, London, or New York; while the exact amount of unearned material wealth which will emasculate individuals in the same society, will vary exactly as their intellectual and moral fibre and natural activity are strong or weak. (It is not uncommon in modern societies to find women of a class relatively very moderately wealthy, the wives and daughters of shopkeepers or professional men, who if their male relations will supply them with a very limited amount of money without exertion on their part, will become as completely parasitic and useless as women with untold wealth at their command.)

The debilitating effect of unlaboured-for wealth lies, then, not in the nature of any material adjunct to life in itself, but in the power it may possess of robbing the individual of all incentive to exertion, thus destroying the intellectual, the physical, and finally, the moral fibre.

In all the civilisations of the past examination will show that almost invariably it has been the female who has tended first to reach this point, and we think examination will show that it has almost invariably been from the woman to the man that enervation and decay have spread.

Why this should be so is obvious. Firstly, it is in the sphere of domestic labour that slave or hired labour most easily and insidiously penetrates. The force of blows or hireling gold can far more easily supply labourers as the preparers of food and clothing, and even as the rearers of children, than it can supply labourers fitted to be entrusted with the toils of war and government, which have in the past been the especial sphere of male toil. The Roman woman had for generations been supplanted in the sphere of her domestic labours and in the toil of rearing and educating her offspring, and had long become abjectly parasitic, before the Roman male had been able to substitute the labour of the hireling and barbarian for his own, in the army, and in the drudgeries of governmental toil.

Secondly, the female having one all-important though passive function which cannot be taken from her, and which is peculiarly connected with her own person, in the act of child-bearing, and her mere sexual attributes being an object of desire and cupidity to the male, she is liable in a peculiarly insidious and gradual manner to become dependent on this one sexual function alone for her support. So much is this the case, that even when she does not in any way perform this function there is still a curious tendency for the kudos of the function still to hang about her, and for her mere potentiality in the direction of a duty which she may never fulfil, to be confused in her own estimation and that of society with the actual fulfilment of that function. Under the mighty aegis of the woman who bears and rears offspring and in other directions labours greatly and actively for her race, creeps in gradually and unnoticed the woman who does none of these things. From the mighty labouring woman who bears human creatures to the full extent of her power, rears her offspring unaided, and performs at the same time severe social labour in other directions (and who is, undoubtedly, wherever found, the most productive toiler known to the race); it is but one step, though a long one, from this woman to the woman who produces offspring freely but does not herself rear them, and performs no compensatory social labour. While from this woman, again, to the one who bears few or no children, but who, whether as a wife or mistress, lives by the exercise of her sex function alone, the step is short. There is but one step farther to the prostitute, who affects no form of productive labour, and who, in place of life, is recognised as producing disease and death, but who exists parasitically through her sexual attribute. Enormous as is the distance between the women at the two extremes of this series, and sharply opposed as their relation to the world is, there is yet, in actual life, no sharp, clear, sudden-drawn line dividing the women of the one type from those of the other. They shade off into each other by delicate and in sensible degrees. And it is down this inclined plane that the women of civilised races are peculiarly tempted, unconsciously, to slip; from the noble height of a condition of the most strenuous social activity, into a condition of complete, helpless, and inactive parasitism, without being clearly aware of the fact themselves, and without society's becoming so—the woman who has ceased to rear her own offspring, or who has ceased to bear offspring at all, and who performs no other productive social function, yet shields

65

the fact from her own eyes by dwelling on the fact that she is a woman, in whom the capacity is at least latent. (There is, indeed, an interesting analogous tendency on the part of the parasitic male, wherever found, to shield his true condition from his own eyes and those of the world by playing at the ancient ancestral forms of male labour. He is almost always found talking loudly of the protection he affords to helpless females and to society, though he is in truth himself protected through the exertion of soldiers, policemen, magistrates, and society generally; and he is almost invariably fond of dangling a sword or other weapon, and wearing some kind of uniform, for the assumption of militarism without severe toil delights him. But it is in a degenerate travesty of the ancient labour of hunting where, at terrible risk to himself, and with endless fatigue, his ancestors supplied the race with its meat and defended it from destruction by wild beasts) that he finds his greatest satisfaction; it serves to render the degradation and uselessness of his existence less obvious to himself and to others than if he passed his life reclining in an armchair.

On Yorkshire moors today may be seen walls of sod, behind which hide certain human males, while hard-labouring men are employed from early dawn in driving birds towards them. As the birds are driven up to him, the hunter behind his wall raises his deadly weapon, and the bird, which it had taken so much human labour to rear and provide, falls dead at his feet; thereby greatly to the increase of the hunter's glory, when, the toils of the chase over, he returns to his city haunts to record his bag. One might almost fancy one saw arise from the heathery turf the shade of some ancient Teutonic ancestor, whose dust has long reposed there, pointing a finger of scorn at his degenerate descendant, as he leers out from behind the sod wall. During the the later Roman Empire, Commodus, in the degenerate days of Rome, at great expense had wild beasts brought from distant lands that he might have the glory of slaying them in the Roman circus; and medals representing himself as Hercules slaying the Nemean lion were struck at his orders. We are not aware that any representation has yet been made in the region of plastic art of the hero of the sod wall; but history repeats itself—and that also may come. It is to be noted that these hunters are not youths, but often ripely adult men, before whom all the lofty enjoyments and employments possible to the male in modern life, lie open.)

These peculiarities in her condition have in all civilised societies laid the female more early and seriously open to the attacks of parasitism than the male. And while the accumulation of wealth has always been the antecedent condition, and the degeneracy and effeteness of the male the final and obvious cause, of the decay of the great dominant races of the past; yet, between these two has always lain, as a great middle term, the parasitism of the female, without which the first would have been inoperative and the last impossible.

Not slavery, nor the most vast accumulations of wealth, could destroy a nation by enervation, whose women remained active, virile, and laborious.

The conception which again and again appears to have haunted successive societies, that it was a possibility for the human male to advance in physical power and intellectual vigour, while his companion female became stationary and inactive, taking no share in the labours of society beyond the passive fulfilment of sexual functions, has always been negated. It has ended as would end the experiment of a man seeking to raise a breed of winning race-horses out of unexercised, short-winded, knock-kneed mares. No, more disastrously! For while the female animal transmits herself to her descendant only or mainly by means of germinal inheritance, and through the influence she may exert over it during gestation, the human female, by producing the intellectual and moral atmosphere in which the early infant years of life are passed, impresses herself far more indelibly on her descendants. Only an able and labouring womanhood can permanently produce an able and labouring manhood; only an effete and inactive male can ultimately be produced by an effete and inactive womanhood. The curled darling, scented and languid, with his drawl, his delicate apparel, his devotion to the rarity and variety of his viands, whose severest labour is the search after pleasure, and for whom even the chase, which was for his remote ancestor an invigorating and manly toil essential for the meat and life of his people, becomes a luxurious and farcical amusement;—this male, whether found in the later Roman Empire, the Turkish harem of today, or in our Northern civilisations, is possible only because generations of parasitic women have preceded him. More repulsive than the parasite female herself, because a yet further product of decay, it is yet only the scent of his mother's boudoir that we smell in his hair. He is like to the bald patches and rotten wool on the back of a scabby sheep; which indeed indicate that, deep beneath the surface, a parasite insect is eating its way into the flesh, but which are not so much the cause of disease, as its final manifestation.

As we have said it is the power of the human female to impress herself on her descendants, male and female, not only through germinal inheritance, through influence during the period of gestation, but above all by producing the mental atmosphere in which the impressionable infant years of life are passed, which makes the condition of the child-bearing female one of paramount interest of the race. It is this fact which causes even prostitution (in many other respects the most repulsive of all the forms of female parasitism which afflicts humanity) to be, probably, not more adverse to the advance and even to the conservation of a healthy and powerful society, than the parasitism of its child-bearing women. For the prostitute, heavily as she weights society for her support, returning disease and mental and emotional disintegration for what she consumes, does not yet so immediately affect the next generation as the kept wife, or kept mistress, who impresses her effete image indelibly on the generations succeeding. (It cannot be too often repeated that the woman who merely bears and brings a child into the world, and then leaves it to be fed and reared by the hands of another, has performed very much less than half of the labour of producing adult humans; in such cases it is the nurse and not the mother who is the most important labourer.)

No man ever yet entered life farther than the length of one navel-cord from the body of the woman who bore him. It is the woman who is the final standard of the race, from which there can be no departure for any distance for any length of time, in any direction: as her brain weakens, weakens the man's she bears; as her muscle softens, softens his; as she decays, decays the people.

Other causes may, and do, lead to the enervation and degeneration of a class or race; the parasitism of its child-bearing women must.

We, the European women of this age, stand today where again and again, in the history of the past, women of other races have stood; but our condition is yet more grave, and of wider import to humanity as a whole than theirs ever was. Let us again consider more closely why this is so.

CHAPTER III

PARASITISM
(*Continued*)

We have seen that, in the past, no such thing as the parasitism of the entire body or large majority of the females inhabiting any territory was possible. Beneath that body of women of the dominant class or race, who did not labour either mentally or physically, there has always been of necessity a far more vast body of females who not only performed the crude physical toil essential to the existence of society before the introduction of mechanical methods of production, but who were compelled to labour the more intensely because there was a parasite class above them to be maintained by their physical toil. The more the female parasite flourished of old, in one class or race, the more certainly all women of other classes or races were compelled to labour only too excessively; and ultimately these females and their descendants were apt to supplant the more enervated class or race. In the absence of machinery and of a vast employment of the motor-forces of nature, parasitism could only threaten a comparatively small section of any community, and a minute section of the human race as a whole. Female parasitism in the past resembled gout—a disease dangerous only to the over-fed, pampered, and few, never to the population of any society as a whole.

At the present day, so enormous has been the advance made in the substitution of mechanical force for crude, physical, human exertion (mechanical force being employed today even in the shaping of feeding-bottles and the creation of artificial foods as substitutes for mother's milk!), that it is now possible not only for a small and wealthy section of women in each civilised community to be maintained without performing any of the ancient, crude, physical labours of their sex, and without depending on the slavery of, or any vast increase in the labour of, other classes of females; but this condition has already been reached, or is tending to be reached, by that large mass of women in civilised societies, who form the intermediate class between poor and rich. During the next fifty years, so rapid will undoubtedly be the spread of the material conditions of civilisation, both in the societies at present civilised and in the societies at present unpermeated by our material civilisation, that the ancient forms of female, domestic, physical labour of even the women of the poorest classes will be little required, their place being taken, not by other females, but by always increasingly perfected labour-saving machinery.

Thus, female parasitism, which in the past threatened only a minute section of earth's women, under existing conditions threatens vast masses, and may, under future conditions, threaten the entire body.

If woman is content to leave to the male all labour in the new and all-important fields which are rapidly opening before the human race; if, as the old forms of domestic labour slip from her for ever and evitably, she does not grasp the new, it is inevitable, that, ultimately, not merely a class, but the whole bodies of females in civilised societies, must sink into a state of more or less absolute dependence on their sexual functions alone. (How real is this apparently very remote danger is interestingly illustrated by a proposition gravely made a few years ago by a man of note in England. He proposed that a compulsory provision should be made for at least the women of the upper and middle classes, by which they might be maintained through life entirely without regard to any productive labour they might perform, not even the passive labour of sexual reproduction being of necessity required of them. That this proposal was received by the women striving to reconstruct the relation of the modern woman to life without acclamation and with scorn, may have surprised its maker; but with no more reason than that man would have for feeling surprise who, seeing a number of persons anxious to escape the infection of some contagious disease, should propose as a cure to inoculate them all with it in its most virulent form!)

As new forms of natural force are mastered and mechanical appliances perfected, it will be quite possible for the male half of all civilised races (and therefore ultimately of all) to absorb the entire fields of intellectual and highly trained manual labour; and it would be entirely possible for the female half of the race, whether as prostitutes, as kept mistresses, or as kept wives, to cease from all forms of active toil, and, as the passive tools of sexual reproduction, or, more decadently still, as the mere instruments of sexual indulgence, to sink into a condition of complete and helpless sex-parasitism.

Sex-parasitism, therefore, presents itself at the end of the nineteenth century and beginning of the twentieth in a guise which it has never before worn. We, the European women of the nineteenth and twentieth centuries, stand therefore in a position the gravity and importance of which was not equalled by that of any of our forerunners in the ancient civilisation. As we master and rise above, or fall and are conquered by, the difficulties of our position, so also will be the future, not merely of our own class, or even of our own race alone, but also of those vast masses who are following on in the wake of our civilisation. The decision we are called on to make is a decision for the race; behind us comes on the tread of incalculable millions of feet.

There is thus no truth in the assertion so often made, even by thoughtful persons, that the male labour question and the woman's question of our day are completely one, and that, would the women of the European race of today but wait peacefully till the males alone had solved their problem, they would find that their own had been solved at the same time.

Were the entire male labour problem of this age satisfactorily settled tomorrow; were all the unemployed or uselessly employed males at both ends of societies, whom the changes of modern civilisation have robbed of their ancient forms of labour, so educated and trained that they were perfectly fitted for the new conditions of life; and were the material benefit and intellectual possibilities, which the substitution of mechanical for human labour now makes possible to humanity, no longer absorbed by the few but dispersed among the whole mass of males in return for their trained labour, yet the woman's problem might be further from satisfactory solution than it is today; and, if it were affected at all, might be affected for the worse. It is wholly untrue that fifty pounds, or two thousand, earned by the male as the result of his physical or mental toil, if part of it be spent by him in supporting non-labouring females, whether as prostitutes, wives, or mistresses, is the same thing to the female or to the race as though that sum had been earned by her own exertion, either directly as wages or indirectly by toiling for the man whose wages supported her. For the moment, truly, the woman so tended lies softer and warmer than had she been compelled to exert herself; ultimately, intellectually, morally, and even physically, the difference in the effect upon her as an individual and on the race is the difference between advance and degradation, between life and death. The increased wealth of the male no more of necessity benefits and raises the female upon whom he expends it, than the increased wealth of his mistress necessarily benefits mentally or physically a poodle because she can give him a down cushion in place of one of feathers, and chicken in place of beef. The wealthier the males of a society become, the greater the temptation, both to themselves and to the females connected with them, to drift toward female parasitism.

The readjustment of the position of the male worker, if it led to a more equitable distribution of wealth among males, might indeed diminish slightly the accompanying tendency to parasitism in the very wealthiest female class; but it would, on the other hand, open up exactly those conditions which make parasitism possible to millions of women today leading healthy and active lives. (The fact cannot be too often dwelt upon that parasitism is not connected with any definite amount of wealth. Any sum supplied to an individual which will so far satisfy him or her as to enable them to live without exertion may absolutely parasitise them; while vast wealth unhealthy as its effects generally tend to be) may, upon certain rare and noble natures, exert hardly any enervating or deleterious influence. An amusing illustration of the different points at which enervation is reached by different females came under our own observation. The wife of an American millionaire was visited by a woman, the daughter and also the widow of small professional men. She stated that she was in need of both food and clothing. The millionaire's wife gave her a leg of mutton and two valuable dresses. The woman proceeded to whine, though in vigorous health, that she had no one to carry them home for her, and could not think of carrying them herself. The American, the descendant of generations of able, labouring, New England, Puritan women, tucked the leg of mutton under one arm and the bundle of clothes under the other and walked off down the city street towards the woman's dwelling, followed by the astonished pauper parasite.

The most helpless case of female degeneration we ever came into contact with was that of a daughter of a poor English officer on half-pay and who had to exist on a few hundreds a year. This woman could neither cook her own food nor make her own clothes, nor was she engaged in any social, political, or intellectual or artistic labour. Though able to dance for a night or play tennis for an afternoon, she was yet hardly able to do her own hair or attire herself, and appeared absolutely to have lost all power of compelling herself to do anything which was at the moment fatiguing or displeasing, as all labour is apt to be, however great its ultimate reward. In a life of twenty-eight years this woman had probably not contributed one hour's earnest toil, mental or physical, to the increase of the sum total of productive human labour. Surrounded with acres of cultivable land, she would possibly have preferred to lie down and die of hunger rather than have cultivated half an acre for food. This is an extreme case; but the ultimate effect of parasitism is always a paralysis of the will and an inability to compel oneself into any course of action for the moment unpleasurable and exhaustive.

That the two problems are not identical is shown, if indeed evidence were needed, by the fact that those males most actively employed in attempting to readjust the relations of the mass of labouring males to the new conditions of life, are sometimes precisely those males who are most bitterly opposed to woman in her attempt to readjust her own position. Not even by the members of those professions, generally regarded as the strongholds of obstructionism and prejudice, has a more short-sighted opposition often been made to the attempts of woman to enter new fields of labour, than have again and again been made by male hand-workers, whether as isolated individuals or in their corporate capacity as trade unions. They have, at least in some certain instances, endeavoured to exclude women, not merely from new fields of intellectual and social labour, but even from those ancient fields of textile manufacture and handicraft, which have through all generations of the past been woman's. The patent and undeniable fact, that where the male labour movement flourishes the woman movement also flourishes, rises not from the fact that they are identical, but that the same healthy and virile condition in a race or society gives rise to both.

As two streams rising from one fountain-head and running a parallel course through long reaches may yet remain wholly distinct, one finding its way satisfactorily to the sea, while the other loses itself in sand or becomes a stagnant marsh, so our modern male and female movements, taking their rise from the same material conditions in modern civilisation, and presenting endless and close analogies with one another in their cause of development, yet remain fundamentally distinct. By both movements the future of the race must be profoundly modified for good or evil; both touch the race in a manner absolutely vital; but both will have to be fought out on their own ground, and independently: and it can be only by determined, conscious, and persistent action on the part of woman that the solution of her own labour problems will proceed co-extensively with that of the other.

How distinct, though similar, is the underlying motive of the two movements, is manifested most clearly by this fact, that, while the male labour movement takes its rise mainly among the poor and hand-labouring classes, where the material pressure of the modern conditions of life fall heaviest, and where the danger of physical suffering and even extinction under that pressure is most felt; the Woman Labour Movement has taken its rise almost as exclusively among the wealthy, cultured, and brain-labouring classes, where alone, at the present day, the danger of enervation through non-employment, and of degeneration through dependence on the sex function exists. The female labour movement of our day is, in its ultimate essence, an endeavour on the part of a section of the race to save itself from inactivity and degeneration, and this, even at the immediate cost of most heavy loss in material comfort and ease to the individuals composing it. The male labour movement is, directly and in the first place, material; and, or at least superficially, more or less self-seeking, though its ultimate reaction on society by saving the poorer members from degradation and dependency and want is undoubtedly wholly social and absolutely essential for the health and continued development of the human race. In the Woman's Labour Movement of our day, which has essentially taken its rise among women of the more cultured and wealthy classes, and which consists mainly in a demand to have the doors leading to professional, political, and highly skilled labour thrown open to them, the ultimate end can only be attained at the cost of more or less intense, immediate, personal suffering and renunciation, though eventually, if brought to a satisfactory conclusion, it will undoubtedly tend to the material and physical well-being of woman herself, as well as to that of her male companions and descendants.

The coming half-century will be a time of peculiar strain, as mankind seeks rapidly to adjust moral ideals and social relationships and the general ordering of life to the new and continually unfolding material conditions. If these two great movements of our age, having this as their object, can be brought into close harmony and co-operation, the readjustment will be the sooner and more painlessly accomplished; but, for the moment, the two movements alike in their origin and alike in many of their methods of procedure, remain distinct.

It is this fact, the consciousness on the part of the women taking their share in the Woman's Movement of our age, that their efforts are not, and cannot be, of immediate advantage to themselves, but that they almost of necessity and immediately lead to loss and renunciation, which gives to this movement its very peculiar tone; setting it apart from the large mass of economic movements, placing it rather in a line with those vast religious developments which at the interval of ages have swept across humanity, irresistibly modifying and reorganising it.

It is the perception of this fact, that, not for herself, nor even for fellow-women alone, but for the benefit of humanity at large, it is necessary she should seek to readjust herself to life, which lends to the modern woman's most superficial and seemingly trivial attempts at readjustment, a certain dignity and importance.

It is this profound hidden conviction which removes from the sphere of the ridiculous the attitude of even the feeblest woman who waves her poor little "Woman's rights" flag on the edge of a platform, and which causes us to forgive even the passionate denunciations, not always wisely thought out, in which she would represent the suffering and evils of woman's condition, as wrongs intentionally inflicted upon her, where they are merely the inevitable results of ages of social movement.

It is this over-shadowing consciousness of a large impersonal obligation, which removes from the sphere of the contemptible and insignificant even the action of the individual young girl, who leaves a home of comfort or luxury for a city garret, where in solitude, and under that stern pressure which is felt by all individuals in arms against the trend of their environment, she seeks to acquire the knowledge necessary for entering on a new form of labour. It is this profound consciousness which makes not less than heroic the figure of the little half-starved student, battling against gigantic odds to take her place beside man in the fields of modern intellectual toil, and which, whether she succeed or fail, makes her a landmark in the course of our human evolution. It is this consciousness of large impersonal ends to be attained, and to the attainment of which each individual is bound to play her part, however small, which removes from the domain of the unnecessary, and raises to importance, the action of each woman who resists the tyranny of fashions in dress or bearing or custom which impedes her in her strife towards the new adjustment.

It is this consciousness which renders almost of solemn import the efforts of the individual female after physical or mental self-culture and expansion; this, which fills with a lofty enthusiasm the heart of the young girl, who, it may be, in some solitary farm-house, in some distant wild of Africa or America, deep into the night bends over her books with the passion and fervour with which an early Christian may have bent over the pages of his Scriptures; feeling that, it may be, she fits herself by each increase of knowledge for she knows not what duties towards the world, in the years to come. It is this consciousness of great impersonal ends, to be brought, even if slowly and imperceptibly, a little nearer by her action, which gives to many a woman strength for renunciation, when she puts from her the lower type of sexual relationship, even if bound up with all the external honour a legal bond can confer, if it offers her only enervation and parasitism; and which enables her often to accept poverty, toil, and sexual isolation (an isolation even more terrible to the woman than to any male), and the renunciation of motherhood, that crowning beatitude of the woman's existence, which, and which alone, fully compensates her for the organic sufferings of womanhood—in the conviction that, by so doing, she makes more possible a fuller and higher attainment of motherhood and wifehood to the women who will follow her. It is this consciousness which makes of solemn importance the knock of the humblest woman at the closed door which shuts off a new field of labour, physical or mental: is she convinced that, not for herself, but in the service of the whole race, she knocks.

It is this abiding consciousness of an end to be attained, reaching beyond her personal life and individual interests, which constitutes the religious element of the Woman's Movement of our day, and binds with the common bond of an impersonal enthusiasm into one solid body the women of whatsoever race, class, and nation who are struggling after the readjustment of woman to life.

This it is also, which in spite of defects and failures on the part of individuals, yet makes the body who these women compose, as a whole, one of the most impressive and irresistible of modern forces. The private soldier of the great victorious army is not always an imposing object as he walks down the village street, cap on side of head and sword dangling between his legs, nor is he always impressive even when he burnishes up his accoutrements or cleans his pannikins; but it is of individuals such as these that the great army is made, which tomorrow, when it is gathered together, may shake the world with its tread.

Possibly not one woman in ten, or even one woman in twenty thousand among those taking part in this struggle, could draw up a clear and succinct account of the causes which have led to the disco-ordination in woman's present position, or give a full account of the benefits to flow from readjustment; as probably not one private soldier in an army of ten or even of twenty thousand, though he is willing to give his life for his land, would yet be able to draw up a clear and succinct account of his land's history in the past and of the conditions which have made war inevitable; and almost as little can he often paint an exact and detailed picture of the benefits to flow from his efts. He knows his land has need of him; he knows his own small place and work.

It is possible that not one woman in ten thousand has grasped with scientific exactitude, and still less could express with verbal sharpness, the great central conditions which yet compel and animate her into action.

Even the great, central fact, that with each generation the entire race passes through the body of its womanhood as through a mould, reappearing with the indelible marks of that mould upon it, that as the os cervix of woman, through which the head of the human infant passes at birth, forms a ring, determining for ever the size at birth of the human head, a size which could only increase if in the course of ages the os cervix of woman should itself slowly expand; and that so exactly the intellectual capacity, the physical vigour, the emotional depth of woman, forms also an untranscendable circle, circumscribing with each successive generation the limits of the expansion of the human race;—even this fact she may not so clearly have grasped intellectually as to be able to throw it into the form of a logical statement. The profound truth, that the continued development of the human race on earth (a development which, as the old myths and dreams of a narrow personal heaven fade from our view, becomes increasingly for many of us the spiritual hope by light of which we continue to live), a development which we hope shall make the humanity of a distant future as much higher in intellectual power and wider in social sympathy than the highest human units of our day, as that is higher than the first primeval ancestor who with quivering limb strove to walk upright and shape his lips to the expression of a word, is possible only if the male and female halves of humanity progress together, expanding side by side in the future as they have done in the past—even this truth it is possible few women have exactly and logically grasped as the basis of their action. The truth that, as the first primitive human males and females, unable to count farther than their fingers, or grasp an abstract idea, or feel the controlling power of social emotion, could only develop into the Sapphos, Aristotles, and Shelleys of a more expanded civilisation, if side by side, and line by line, male and female forms have expanded together; if, as the convolutions of his brain increased in complexity, so increased the convolutions in hers; if, as her forehead grew higher, so developed his; and that, if the long upward march of the future is ever to be accomplished by the race, male and female must march side by side, acting and reacting on each other through inheritance; or progress is impossible. The truth that, as the existence of even the male Bushman would be impossible without the existence of the analogous Bushwoman with the same gifts; and that as races which can produce among their males a William Kingdon Clifford, a Tolstoy, or a Robert Browning, would be inconceivable and impossible, unless among its females it could also produce a Sophia Kovalevsky, a George Eliot, or a Louise Michel; so, also, in the future, that higher and more socialised human race we dream of can only come into existence, because in both the sex forms have evolved together, now this sex and then that, so to speak, catching up the ball of life and throwing it back to the other, slightly if imperceptibly enlarging and beautifying it as it passes through their hands. The fact that without the reaction of interevolution between the sexes, there can be no real and permanent human advance; without the enlarged deep-thinking Eve to bear him, no enlarged Adam; without the enlarged widely sympathising Adam to beget her, no enlarged widely comprehending Eve; without an enlarged Adam and an enlarged Eve, no enlarged and beautified generation of mankind on earth; that an arrest in one form is an arrest in both; and in the upward march of the entire human family. The truth that, if at the present day, woman, after her long upward march side by side with man, developing with him through the countless ages, by means of the endless exercise of the faculties of mind and body, has now, at last, reached her ultimate limit of growth, and can progress no farther; that, then, here also, today, the growth of the human spirit is to be stayed; that here, on the spot of woman's arrest, is the standard of the race to be finally planted, to move forward no more, for ever:— that, if the parasite woman on her couch, loaded with gewgaws, the plaything and amusement of man, be the permanent and final manifestation of female human life on the globe, then that couch is also the death-bed of human evolution. These profound underlying truths, perhaps, not one woman in twenty thousand of those actively engaged in the struggle for readjustment has so closely and keenly grasped that she can readily throw them into the form of exact language; and yet, probably, not the feeblest woman taking share in our endeavour toward readjustment and expansion fails to be animated by a vague but profound consciousness of their existence. Beyond the small evils, which she seeks by her immediate, personal action to remedy, lie, she feels; large ills of which they form but an off-shoot; beyond the small good which she seeks to effect, lies, she believes, a great and universal beatitude to be attained; beyond the little struggle of today, lies the larger struggle of the centuries, in which neither she alone nor her sex alone are concerned, but all mankind.

That such should be the mental attitude of the average woman taking part in the readjustive sexual movement of today; that so often on the public platform and in literature adduces merely secondary arguments, and is wholly unable logically to give an account of the great propelling conditions behind it, is sometimes taken as an indication of the inefficiency, and probably the ultimate failure, of the movement in which she takes part. But in truth, that is not so. It is rather an indication which shows how healthy, and deeply implanted in the substance of human life, are the roots of this movement; and it places it in a line with all those vast controlling movements which have in the course of the ages reorganised human life.

For those great movements which have permanently modified the condition of humanity have never taken their rise amid the chopped logic of schools; they have never drawn their vitality from a series of purely intellectual and abstract inductions. They have arisen always through the action of widely spread material and spiritual conditions, creating widespread human needs; which, pressing upon the isolated individuals, awakens at last continuous, if often vague and uncertain, social movement in a given direction. Mere intellectual comprehension may guide, retard, or accelerate the great human movements; it has never created them. It may even be questioned whether those very leaders, who have superficially appeared to create and organise great and successful social movements, have themselves, in most cases, perhaps in any, fully understood in all their complexity the movements they themselves have appeared to rule. They have been, rather, themselves permeated by the great common need; and being possessed of more will, passion, intensity, or intellect, they have been able to give voice to that which in others was dumb, and conscious direction to that which in others was unconscious desire: they have been but the foremost crest of a great wave of human necessity: they have not themselves created the wave which bears themselves, and humanity, onwards. The artificial social movements which have had their origin in the arbitrary will of individuals, guided with however much determination and reason, have of necessity proved ephemeral and abortive. An Alexander might will to weld a Greece and an Asia into one; a Napoleon might resolve to create of a diversified Europe one consolidated state; and by dint of skill and determination they might for a moment appear to be accomplishing that which they desired; but the constraining individual will being withdrawn, the object of their toil has melted away, as the little heap of damp sand gathered under the palm of a child's hand on the sea-shore, melts away, scattered by the wind and washed out by the waves, the moment the hand that shaped it is withdrawn; while the small, soft, indefinite, watery fragment of jelly-fish lying beside it, though tossed hither and thither by water and wind, yet retains its shape and grows, because its particles are bound by an internal and organic force.

Our woman's movement resembles strongly, in this matter, the gigantic religious and intellectual movement which for centuries convulsed the life of Europe; and had, as its ultimate outcome, the final emancipation of the human intellect and the freedom of the human spirit. Looked back upon from the vantage-point of the present, this past presents the appearance of one vast, steady, persistent movement proceeding always in one ultimate direction, as though guided by some controlling human intellect. But, to the mass of human individuals taking part in it, it presented an appearance far otherwise. It was fought out, now here, now there, by isolated individuals and small groups, and often for what appeared small and almost personal ends, having sometimes, superficially, little in common. Now it was a Giordano Bruno, burnt in Rome in defence of abstract theory with regard to the nature of the First Cause; then an Albigense hurled from his rocks because he refused to part with the leaves of his old Bible; now a Dutch peasant woman, walking serenely to the stake because she refused to bow her head before two crossed rods; then a Servetus burnt by Protestant Calvin at Geneva; or a Spinoza cut off from his tribe and people because he could see nothing but God anywhere; and then it was an exiled Rousseau or Voltaire, or a persecuted Bradlaugh; till, in our own day the last sounds of the long fight are dying about us, as fading echoes, in the guise of a few puerile attempts to enforce trivial disabilities on the ground of abstract convictions. The vanguard of humanity has won its battle for freedom of thought.

But, to the men and women taking part in that mighty movement during the long centuries of the past, probably nothing was quite clear, in the majority of cases, but their own immediate move. Not the leaders—most certainly not good old Martin Luther, even when he gave utterance to his immortal "I can no otherwise" (the eternal justification of all reformers and social innovators!), understood the whole breadth of the battlefield on which they were engaged, or grasped with precision the issues which were involved. The valiant Englishman, who, as the flames shot up about him, cried to his companion in death, "Play the man, Master Ridley; we shall by God's grace this day light such a candle in England, as shall never be put out!" undoubtedly believed that the candle lighted was the mere tallow rushlight of a small sectarian freedom for England alone; nor perceived that what he lighted was but one ray of the vast, universal aurora of intellectual and spiritual liberty, whose light was ultimately to stream, not only across England, but across the earth. Nevertheless, undoubtedly, behind all these limited efforts, for what appeared, superficially, limited causes, lay, in the hearts of the men and women concerned, through the ages, a profound if vague consciousness of ends larger than they clearly knew, to be subserved by their action; of a universal social duty and a great necessity.

That the Woman's Movement of our day has not taken its origin from any mere process of theoretic argument; that it breaks out, now here and now there, in forms divergent and at times superficially almost irreconcilable; that the majority of those taking part in it are driven into action as the result of the immediate pressure of the conditions of life, and are not always able logically to state the nature of all causes which propel them, or to paint clearly all results of their action; so far from removing it from the category of the vast reorganising movements of humanity, places it in a line with them, showing how vital, spontaneous, and wholly organic and unartificial is its nature.

The fact that, at one point, it manifests itself in a passionate, and at times almost incoherent, cry for an accredited share in public and social duties; while at another it makes itself felt as a determined endeavour after self-culture; that in one land it embodies itself mainly in a resolute endeavour to enlarge the sphere of remunerative labour for women; while in another it manifests itself chiefly as an effort to recoordinate the personal relation of the sexes; that in one individual it manifests itself as a passionate and sometimes noisy struggle for liberty of personal action; while in another it is being fought out silently in the depth of the individual consciousness—that primal battleground, in which all questions of reform and human advance must ultimately be fought and decided;—all this diversity, and the fact that the average woman is entirely concerned in labour in her own little field, shows, not the weakness, but the strength of the movement; which, taken as a whole, is a movement steady and persistent in one direction, the direction of increased activity and culture, and towards the negation of all possibility of parasitism in the human female. Slowly, and unconsciously, as the child is shaped in the womb, this movement shapes itself in the bosom of our time, taking its place beside those vast human developments, of which men, noting their spontaneity and the co-ordination of their parts, have said, in the phraseology of old days, "This thing is not of man, but of God."

He who today looks at some great Gothic cathedral in its final form, seems to be looking at that which might have been the incarnation of the dream of some single soul of genius. But in truth, its origin was far otherwise. Ages elapsed from the time the first rough stone was laid as a foundation till the last spire and pinnacle were shaped, and the hand which laid the foundation-stone was never the same as that which set the last stone upon the coping. Generations often succeeded one another, labouring at gargoyle, rose-window, and shaft, and died, leaving the work to others; the master-builder who drew up the first rough outline passed away, and was succeeded by others, and the details of the work as completed bore sometimes but faint resemblance to the work as he devised it; no man fully understood all that others had done or were doing, but each laboured in his place; and the work as completed had unity; it expressed not the desire and necessity of one mind, but of the human spirit of that age; and not less essential to the existence of the building was the labour of the workman who passed a life

86

of devotion in carving gargoyles or shaping rose-windows, than that of the greatest master who drew general outlines: perhaps it was yet more heroic; for, for the master-builder, who, even if it were but vaguely, had an image of what the work would be when the last stone was laid and the last spire raised, it was easy to labour with devotion and zeal, though well he might know that the placing of that last stone and the raising of that last spire would not be his, and that the building in its full beauty and strength he should never see; but for the journeyman labourer who carried on his duties and month by month toiled at carving his own little gargoyle or shaping the traceries in his own little oriel window, without any complete vision, it was not so easy; nevertheless, it was through the conscientious labours of such alone, through their heaps of chipped and spoiled stones, which may have lain thick about them, that at the last the pile was reared in its strength and beauty.

For a Moses who could climb Pisgah, and, though it were through a mist of bitter tears, could see stretching before him the land of the inheritance, a land which his feet should never tread and whose fruit his hand should never touch, it was yet, perhaps, not so hard to turn round and die; for, as in a dream, he had seen the land: but for the thousands who could climb no Pisgah, who were to leave their bones whitening in the desert, having even from afar never seen the true outline of the land; those who, on that long march, had not even borne the Ark nor struck the timbrel, but carried only their small household vessels and possessions, for these it was perhaps not so easy to lie down and perish in the desert, knowing only that far ahead somewhere, lay a Land of Promise. Nevertheless, it was by the slow and sometimes wavering march of such as these, that the land was reached by the people at last.

For her, whose insight enables her to see, through the distance, those large beatitudes towards which the struggles and suffering of the women of today may tend; who sees beyond the present, though in a future which she knows she will never enter, an enlarged and strengthened womanhood bearing forward with it a strengthened and expanded race, it is not so hard to renounce and labour with unshaken purpose: but for those who have not that view, and struggle on, animated at most by a vague consciousness that somewhere ahead lies a large end, towards which their efforts tend; who labour year after year at some poor little gargoyle of a Franchise Bill, or the shaping of some rough little foundation-stone of reform in education, or dress a stone (which perhaps never quite fits the spot it was intended for, and has to be thrown aside!); or who carve away all their lives to produce a corbel of some reform in sexual relations, in the end to find it break under the chisel; who, out of many failures attain, perhaps, to no success, or but to one, and that so small and set so much in the shade that no eye will ever see it; for such as these, it is perhaps not so easy to labour without growing weary. Nevertheless, it is through the labours of these myriad toilers, each working in her own minute sphere, with her own small outlook, and out of endless failures and miscarriages, that at last the enwidened and beautified relations of woman to life must rise, if they are ever to come.

When a starfish lies on the ground at the bottom of a sloping rock it has to climb, it seems to the onlooker as though there were nothing which could stir the inert mass and no means for taking it to the top. Yet watch it. Beneath its lower side, hidden from sight, are a million fine tentacles; impulses of will from the central nerve radiate throughout the whole body, and each tiny fibre, fine as a hair, slowly extends itself, and seizes on the minute particle of rough rock nearest to it; now a small tentacle slips its hold, and then it holds firmly, and then slowly and slowly the whole inert mass rises to the top.

It is often said of those who lead in this attempt at the readaption of woman's relation to life, that they are "New Women"; and they are at times spoken of as though they were a something portentous and unheard-of in the order of human life.

But, the truth is, we are not new. We who lead in this movement today are of that old, old Teutonic womanhood, which twenty centuries ago ploughed its march through European forests and morasses beside its male companion; which marched with the Cimbri to Italy, and with the Franks across the Rhine, with the Varagians into Russia, and the Alamani into Switzerland; which peopled Scandinavia, and penetrated to Britain; whose priestesses had their shrines in German forests, and gave out the oracle for peace or war. We have in us the blood of a womanhood that was never bought and never sold; that wore no veil, and had no foot bound; whose realised ideal of marriage was sexual companionship and an equality in duty and labour; who stood side by side with the males they loved in peace or war, and whose children, when they had borne them, sucked manhood from their breasts, and even through their foetal existence heard a brave heart beat above them. We are women of a breed whose racial ideal was no Helen of Troy, passed passively from male hand to male hand, as men pass gold or lead; but that Brynhild whom Segurd found, clad in helm and byrne, the warrior maid, who gave him counsel "the deepest that ever yet was given to living man," and "wrought on him to the performing of great deeds;" who, when he died, raised high the funeral pyre and lay down on it beside him, crying, "Nor shall the door swing to at the heel of him as I go in beside him!" We are of a race of women that of old knew no fear, and feared no death, and lived great lives and hoped great hopes; and if today some of us have fallen on evil and degenerate times, there moves in us yet the throb of the old blood.

If it be today on no physical battlefield that we stand beside our men, and on no march through no external forest or morass that we have to lead; it is yet the old spirit which, undimmed by two thousand years, stirs within us in deeper and subtler ways; it is yet the cry of the old, free Northern woman which makes the world today. Though the battlefield be now for us all, in the laboratory or the workshop, in the forum or the study, in the assembly and in the mart and the political arena, with the pen and not the sword, of the head and not the arm, we still stand side by side with the men we love, "to dare with them in war and to suffer with them in peace," as the Roman wrote of our old Northern womanhood.

Those women, of whom the old writers tell us, who, barefooted and white robed, led their Northern hosts on that long march to Italy, were animated by the thought that they led their people to a land of warmer sunshine and richer fruitage; we, today, believe we have caught sight of a land bathed in a nobler than any material sunlight, with a fruitage richer than any which the senses only can grasp: and behind us, we believe there follows a longer train than any composed of our own race and people; the sound of the tread we hear behind us is that of all earth's women, bearing within them the entire race. The footpath, yet hardly perceptible, which we tread down today, will, we believe, be life's broadest and straightest road, along which the children of men will pass to a higher co-ordination and harmony. The banner which we unfurl today is not new: it is the standard of the old, free, monogamous, labouring woman, which, twenty hundred years ago, floated over the forests of Europe. We shall bear it on, each generation as it falls passing it into the hand of that which follows, till we plant it so high that all nations of the world shall see it; till the women of the humblest human races shall be gathered beneath its folds, and no child enter life that was not born within its shade.

We are not new! If you would understand us, go back two thousand years, and study our descent; our breed is our explanation. We are the daughters of our fathers as well as of our mothers. In our dreams we still hear the clash of the shields of our forefathers as they struck them together before battle and raised the shout of "Freedom!" In our dreams it is with us still, and when we wake it breaks from our own lips! We are the daughters of those men.

But, it may be said, "Are there not women among you who

would use the shibboleth, of freedom and labour, merely as a means for opening a door to a greater and more highly flavoured self-indulgence, to a more lucrative and enjoyable parasitism? Are there not women who, under the guise of 'work,' are seeking only increased means of sensuous pleasure and self-indulgence; to whom intellectual training and the opening to new fields of labour side by side with man, mean merely new means of self-advertisement and parasitic success?" We answer: There may be such, truly; among us—but not of us! This at least is true, that we, ourselves, are seldom deceived by them; the sheep generally recognise the wolf however carefully fitted the sheepskin under which he hides, though the onlookers may not; and though not always be able to drive him from the flock! The outer world may be misled; we, who stand shoulder to shoulder with them, know them; they are not many; neither are they new. They are one of the oldest survivals, and among the most primitive relics in the race. They are as old as Loki among the gods, as Lucifer among the Sons of the Morning, as the serpent in the Garden of Eden, as pain and dislocation in the web of human life.

Such women are as old as that first primitive woman who, when she went with her fellows to gather wood for the common household, put grass in the centre of the bundle that she might appear to carry as much as they, yet carry nothing; she is as old as the first man who threw away his shield in battle, and yet, when it was over, gathered with the victors to share the spoils, as old as cowardice and lust in the human and animal world; only to cease from being when, perhaps, an enlarged and expanded humanity shall have cast the last slough of its primitive skin.

Every army has its camp-followers, not among its accredited soldiers, but who follow in its train, ready to attack and rifle the fallen on either side. To lookers on, they may appear soldiers; but the soldier knows who they are. At the Judean supper there was one Master, and to the onlooker there may have seemed twelve apostles; in truth only twelve were of the company, and one was not of it. There has always been this thirteenth figure at every sacramental gathering, since the world began, wherever the upholders of a great cause have broken spiritual bread; but it may be questioned whether in any instance this thirteenth figure has been able to destroy, or even vitally to retard, any great human movement. Judas could hang his Master by a kiss; but he could not silence the voice which for a thousand years rang out of that Judean grave. Again and again, in social, political, and intellectual movements, the betrayer betrays;—and the cause marches on over the body of the man.

There are women, as there are men, whose political, social, intellectual, or philanthropic labours are put on, as the harlot puts on paint, and for the same purpose: but they can no more retard the progress of the great bulk of vital and sincere womanhood, than the driftwood on the surface of a mighty river can ultimately prevent its waters from reaching the sea.

CHAPTER IV

WOMAN AND WAR

But it may also be said, "Granting fully that you are right, that, as woman's old fields of labour slip from her, she must grasp the new, or must become wholly dependent on her sexual function alone, all the other elements of human nature in her becoming atrophied and arrested through lack of exercise: and, granting that her evolution being arrested, the evolution of the whole race will be also arrested in her person: granting all this to the full, and allowing that the bulk of human labour tends to become more and more intellectual and less and less purely mechanical, as perfected machinery takes the place of crude human exertion; and that therefore if woman is to be saved from degeneration and parasitism, and the body of humanity from arrest, she must receive a training which will cultivate all the intellectual and all the physical faculties with which she is endowed, and be allowed freely to employ them; nevertheless, would it not be possible, and perhaps be well, that a dividing line of some kind should be drawn between the occupations of men and of women? Would it not, for example, be possible that woman should retain agriculture, textile manufacture, trade, domestic management, the education of youth, and medicine, in addition to child-bearing, as her exclusive fields of toil; while, to the male, should be left the study of abstract science, law and war, and statecraft; as of old, man took war and the chase, and woman absorbed the further labours of life? Why should there not be again a fair and even division in the field of social labour?"

Superficially, this suggestion appears rational, having at least this to recommend it, that it appears to harmonise with the course of human evolution in the past; but closely examined, it will, we think, be found to have no practical or scientific basis, and to be out of harmony with the conditions of modern life. In ancient and primitive societies, the mere larger size and muscular strength of man, and woman's incessant physical activity in child-bearing and suckling and rearing the young, made almost inevitable a certain sexual division of labour in almost all countries, save perhaps in ancient Egypt. (The division of labour between the sexes in Ancient Egypt and other exceptional countries, is a matter of much interest, which cannot here be entered on.) Woman naturally took the heavy agricultural and domestic labours, which were yet more consistent with the continual dependence of infant life on her own, than those of man in war and the chase. There was nothing artificial in such a division; it threw the heaviest burden of the most wearying and unexciting forms of social labour on woman, but under it both sexes laboured in a manner essential to the existence of society, and each transmitted to the other, through inheritance, the fruit of its slowly expanding and always exerted powers; and the race progressed.

Individual women might sometimes, and even often, become the warrior chief of a tribe; the King of Ashantee might train his terrible regiment of females; and men might now and again plant and weave for their children: but in the main, and in most societies, the division of labour was just, natural, beneficial; and it was inevitable that such a division should take place. Were today a band of civilised men, women, and infants thrown down absolutely naked and defenceless in some desert, and cut off hopelessly from all external civilised life, undoubtedly very much the old division of labour would, at least for a time, reassert itself; men would look about for stones and sticks with which to make weapons to repel wild beasts and enemies, and would go a-hunting meat and fighting savage enemies and tend the beasts when tamed: (The young captured animals would

94

probably be tamed and reared by the women.) women would suckle their children, cook the meat men brought, build shelters, look for roots and if possible cultivate them; there certainly would be no parasite in the society; the woman who refused to labour for her offspring, and the man who refused to hunt or defend society, would not be supported by their fellows, would soon be extinguished by want. As wild beasts were extinguished and others tamed and the materials for war improved, fewer men would be needed for hunting and war; then they would remain at home and aid in building and planting; many women would retire into the house to perfect domestic toil and handicrafts, and on a small scale the common ancient evolution of society would probably practically repeat itself. But for the present, we see no such natural and spontaneous division of labour based on natural sexual distinctions in the new fields of intellectual or delicately skilled manual labour, which are taking the place of the old.

It is possible, though at present there is nothing to give indication of such a fact, and it seems highly improbable, that, in some subtle manner now incomprehensible, there might tend to be a subtle correlation between that condition of the brain and nervous system which accompanies ability in the direction of certain modern forms of mental, social labour, and the particular form of reproductive function possessed by an individual. It may be that, inexplicable as it seems, there may ultimately be found to be some connection between that condition of the brain and nervous system which fits the individual for the study of the higher mathematics, let us say, and the nature of their sex attributes. The mere fact that, of the handful of women who, up to the present, have received training and been allowed to devote themselves to abstract study, several have excelled in the higher mathematics, proves of necessity no pre-eminent tendency on the part of the female sex in the direction of mathematics, as compared to labour in the fields of statesmanship, administration, or law; as into these fields there has been practically no admittance for women. It is sometimes stated, that as several women of genius in modern times have sought to find expression for their creative powers in the art of fiction, there must be some inherent connection in the human brain between the ovarian sex function and the art of fiction. The fact is, that modern fiction being merely a description of human life in any of its phases, and being the only art that can be exercised without special training or special appliances, and produced in the moments stolen from the multifarious, brain-destroying occupations which fill the average woman's life, they have been driven to find this outlet for their powers as the only one presenting itself. How far otherwise might have been the directions in which their genius would naturally have expressed itself can be known only partially even to the women themselves; what the world has lost by that compulsory expression of genius, in a form which may not have been its most natural form of expression, or only one of its forms, no one can ever know. Even in the little third-rate novelist whose works cumber the ground, we see often a pathetic figure, when we recognise that beneath that failure in a complex and difficult art, may lie buried a sound legislator, an able architect, an original scientific investigator, or a good judge. Scientifically speaking, it is as unproven that there is any organic relation between the brain of the female and the production of art in the form of fiction, as that there is an organic relation between the hand of woman and a typewriting machine. Both the creative writer and the typist, in their respective spheres, are merely finding outlets for their powers in the direction of least resistance. The tendency of women at the present day to undertake certain forms of labour, proves only that in the crabbed, walled-in, and bound conditions surrounding woman at the present day, these are the lines along which action is most possible to her.

It may possibly be that in future ages, when the male and female forms have been placed in like intellectual conditions, with like stimuli, like training, and like rewards, that some aptitudes may be found running parallel with the line of sex function when humanity is viewed as a whole. It may possibly be that, when the historian of the future looks back over the history of the intellectually freed and active sexes for countless generations, that a decided preference of the female intellect for mathematics, engineering, or statecraft may be made clear; and that a like marked inclination in the male to excel in acting, music, or astronomy may by careful and large comparison be shown. But, for the present, we have no adequate scientific data from which to draw any conclusion, and any attempt to divide the occupations in which male and female intellects and wills should be employed, must be to attempt a purely artificial and arbitrary division: a division not more rational and scientific than an attempt to determine by the colour of his eyes and the shape and strength of his legs, whether a lad should be an astronomer or an engraver. Those physical differences among mankind which divide races and nations—not merely those differences, enormously greater as they are generally, than any physical differences between male and female of the same race, which divide the Jew and the Swede, the Japanese and the Englishman, but even those subtle physical differences which divide closely allied races such as the English and German—often appear to be allied with certain subtle differences in intellectual aptitudes. Yet even with regard to these differences, it is almost impossible to determine scientifically in how far they are the result of national traditions, environment, and education, and in how far the result of real differences in organic conformation. (In thinking of physical sex differences, the civilised man of modern times has always to guard himself against being unconsciously misled by the very exaggerated external sex differences which our unnatural method of sex clothing and dressing the hair produces. The unclothed and natural human male and female bodies are not more divided from each other than those of the lion and lioness. Our remote Saxon ancestors, with their great, almost naked, white bodies and flowing hair worn long by

97

both sexes, were but little distinguished from each other; while among their modern descendants the short hair, darkly clothed, manifestly two-legged male differs absolutely from the usually long-haired, colour bedizened, much beskirted female. Were the structural differences between male and female really one half as marked as the artificial visual differences, they would be greater than those dividing, not merely any species of man from another, but as great as those which divide orders in the animal world. Only a mind exceedingly alert and analytical can fail ultimately to be misled by habitual visual misrepresentation. There is not, probably, one man or woman in twenty thousand who is not powerfully influenced in modern life in their conception of the differences, physical and intellectual, dividing the human male and female, by the grotesque exaggerations of modern attire and artificial manners.)

No study of the mere physical differences between individuals of different races would have enabled us to arrive at any knowledge of their mental aptitude; nor does the fact that certain individuals of a given human variety have certain aptitudes form a rational ground for compelling all individuals of that variety to undertake a certain form of labour.

No analysis, however subtle, of the physical conformation of the Jew could have suggested a priori, and still less could have proved, apart from ages of practical experience, that, running parallel with any physical characteristics which may distinguish him from his fellows, was an innate and unique intellectual gift in the direction of religion. The fact that, during three thousand years, from Moses to Isaiah, through Jesus and Paul on to Spinoza, the Jewish race has produced men who have given half the world its religious faith and impetus, proves that, somewhere and somehow, whether connected organically with that physical organisation that marks the Jew, or as the result of his traditions and training, there does go this gift in the matter of religion. Yet, on the other hand, we find millions of Jews who are totally and markedly deficient in it, and to base any practical legislation for the individual even on this proven intellectual aptitude of the race as a whole would be manifestly as ridiculous as abortive. Yet more markedly, with the German—no consideration of his physical peculiarities, though it proceeded to the subtlest analysis of nerve, bone, and muscle, could in the present stage of our knowledge have proved to us what generations of experience appear to have proved, that, with that organisation which constitutes the German, goes an unique aptitude for music. There is always the possibility of mistaking the result of training and external circumstance for inherent tendency, but when we consider the passion for music which the German has shown, and when we consider that the greatest musicians the world has seen, from Bach, Beethoven, and Mozart to Wagner, have been of that race, it appears highly probable that such a correlation between the German organisation and the intellectual gift of music does exist. Similar intellectual peculiarities seem to be connoted by the external differences which mark off other races from each other. Nevertheless, were persons of all of these nationalities gathered in one colony, any attempt to legislate for their restriction to certain forms of intellectual labour on the ground of their apparently proved national aptitudes or disabilities, would be regarded as insane. To insist that all Jews, and none but Jews, should lead and instruct in religious matters; that all Englishmen, and none but Englishmen, should engage in trade; that each German should make his living by music, and none but a German allowed to practise it, would drive to despair the unfortunate individual Englishman, whose most marked deficiency might be in the direction of finance and bartering trade power; the Jew, whose religious instincts might be entirely rudimentary; or the German, who could not distinguish one note from another; and the society as a whole would be an irremediable loser, in one of the heaviest of all forms of social loss—the loss of the full use of the highest capacities of all its members.

It may be that with sexes as with races, the subtlest physical difference between them may have their fine mental correlatives; but no abstract consideration of the human body in relation to its functions of sex can, in the present state of our knowledge, show us what intellectual capacities tend to vary with sexual structure, and nothing in the present or past condition of male and female give us more than the very faintest possible indication of the relation of their intellectual aptitudes and their sexual functions. And even were it proved by centuries of experiment that with the possession of the uterine function of sex tends to go exceptional intellectual capacity in the direction of mathematics rather than natural history, or an inclination for statecraft rather than for mechanical invention; were it proved that, generally speaking and as a whole, out of twenty thousand women devoting themselves to law and twenty thousand to medicine, they tended to achieve relatively more in the field of law than of medicine, there would yet be no possible healthy or rational ground for restricting the activities of the individual female to that line in which the average female appeared rather more frequently to excel. (Minds not keenly analytical are always apt to mistake mere correlation of appearance with causative sequence. We have heard it gravely asserted that between potatoes, pigs, mud cabins and Irishmen there was an organic connection: but we who have lived in Colonies, know that within two generations the pure-bred descendant of the mud cabiner becomes often the successful politician, wealthy financier, or great judge; and shows no more predilection for potatoes, pigs, and mud cabins than men of any other race.)

That even one individual in a society should be debarred from undertaking that form of social toil for which it is most fitted, makes an unnecessary deficit in the general social assets. That one male Froebel should be prohibited or hampered in his labour as an educator of infancy, on the ground that infantile instruction was the field of the female; that one female with gifts in the direction of state administration, should be compelled to instruct an infants' school, perhaps without the slightest gift for so doing, is a running to waste of social life-blood.

Free trade in labour and equality of training, intellectual or physical, is essential if the organic aptitudes of a sex or class are to be determined. And our demand today is that natural conditions, inexorably, but beneficently, may determine the labours of each individual, and not artificial restrictions.

As there is no need to legislate that Hindus, being generally supposed to have a natural incapacity for field sports, shall not betake themselves to them—for, if they have no capacity, they will fail; and, as in spite of the Hindus' supposed general incapacity for sport, it is possible for an individual Hindu to become the noted batsman of his age; so, also, there is no need to legislate that women should be restricted in her choice of fields of labour; for the organic incapacity of the individual, if it exist, will legislate far more powerfully than any artificial, legal, or social obstruction can do; and it may be that the one individual in ten thousand who selects a field not generally sought by his fellows will enrich humanity by the result of an especial genius. Allowing all to start from the one point in the world of intellectual culture and labour, with our ancient Mother Nature sitting as umpire, distributing the prizes and scratching from the lists the incompetent, is all we demand, but we demand it determinedly. Throw the puppy into the water: if it swims, well; if it sinks, well; but do not tie a rope round its throat and weight it with a brick, and then assert its incapacity to keep afloat.

For the present our cry is, "We take all labour for our province!"

From the judge's seat to the legislator's chair; from the statesman's closet to the merchant's office; from the chemist's laboratory to the astronomer's tower, there is no post or form of toil for which it is not our intention to attempt to fit ourselves; and there is no closed door we do not intend to force open; and there is no fruit in the garden of knowledge it is not our determination to eat. Acting in us, and through us, nature we know will mercilessly expose to us our deficiencies in the field of human toil, and reveal to us our powers. And, for today, we take all labour for our province!

But, it may then be said: "What of war, that struggle of the human creature to attain its ends by physical force and at the price of the life of others: will you take part in that also?" We reply: Yes; more particularly in that field we intend to play our part. We have always borne part of the weight of war, and the major part. It is not merely that in primitive times we suffered from the destruction of the fields we tilled and the houses we built; or that in later times as domestic labourers and producers, though unwaged, we, in taxes and material loss and additional labour, paid as much as our males towards the cost of war; nor is it that in a comparatively insignificant manner, as nurses of the wounded in modern times, or now and again as warrior chieftainesses and leaders in primitive and other societies, we have borne our part; nor is it even because the spirit of resolution in its women, and their willingness to endure, has in all ages again and again largely determined the fate of a race that goes to war, that we demand our controlling right where war is concerned. Our relation to war is far more intimate, personal, and indissoluble than this. Men have made boomerangs, bows, swords, or guns with which to destroy one another; we have made the men who destroyed and were destroyed! We have in all ages produced, at an enormous cost, the primal munition of war, without which no other would exist. There is no battlefield on earth, nor ever has been, howsoever covered with slain, which is has not cost the women of the race more in actual bloodshed and anguish to supply, then it has cost the men who lie there. We pay the first cost on all human life.

In supplying the men for the carnage of a battlefield, women have not merely lost actually more blood, and gone through a more acute anguish and weariness, in the long months of bearing and in the final agony of childbirth, than has been experienced by the men who cover it; but, in the long months and years of rearing that follow, the women of the race go through a long, patiently endured strain which no knapsacked soldier on his longest march has ever more than equalled; while, even in the matter of death, in all civilised societies, the probability that the average woman will die in childbirth is immeasurably greater than the probability that the average male will die in battle.

There is, perhaps, no woman, whether she have borne children, or be merely potentially a child-bearer, who could look down upon a battlefield covered with slain, but the thought would rise in her, "So many mothers' sons! So many bodies brought into the world to lie there! So many months of weariness and pain while bones and muscles were shaped within; so many hours of anguish and struggle that breath might be; so many baby mouths drawing life at woman's breasts;—all this, that men might lie with glazed eyeballs, and swollen bodies, and fixed, blue, unclosed mouths, and great limbs tossed—this, that an acre of ground might be manured with human flesh, that next year's grass or poppies or karoo bushes may spring up greener and redder, where they have lain, or that the sand of a plain may have a glint of white bones!" And we cry, "Without an inexorable cause, this should not be!" No woman who is a woman says of a human body, "It is nothing!"

On that day, when the woman takes her place beside the man in the governance and arrangement of external affairs of her race will also be that day that heralds the death of war as a means of arranging human differences. No tinsel of trumpets and flags will ultimately seduce women into the insanity of recklessly destroying life, or gild the wilful taking of life with any other name than that of murder, whether it be the slaughter of the million or of one by one. And this will be, not because with the sexual function of maternity necessarily goes in the human creature a deeper moral insight, or a loftier type of social instinct than that which accompanies the paternal. Men have in all ages led as nobly as women in many paths of heroic virtue, and toward the higher social sympathies; in certain ages, being freer and more widely cultured, they have led further and better. The fact that woman has no inherent all-round moral superiority over her male companion, or naturally on all points any higher social instinct, is perhaps most clearly exemplified by one curious very small fact: the two terms signifying intimate human relationships which in almost all human languages bear the most sinister and antisocial significance are both terms which have as their root the term "mother," and denote feminine relationships—the words "mother-in-law" and "step-mother."

In general humanity, in the sense of social solidarity, and in magnanimity, the male has continually proved himself at least the equal of the female.

Nor will women shrink from war because they lack courage. Earth's women of every generation have faced suffering and death with an equanimity that no soldier on a battlefield has ever surpassed and few have equalled; and where war has been to preserve life, or land, or freedom, unparasitised and labouring women have in all ages known how to bear an active part, and die.

Nor will woman's influence militate against war because in the future woman will not be able physically to bear her part in it. The smaller size of her muscle, which would severely have disadvantaged her when war was conducted with a battle-axe or sword and hand to hand, would now little or at all affect her. If intent on training for war, she might acquire the skill for guiding a Maxim or shooting down a foe with a Lee-Metford at four thousand yards as ably as any male; and undoubtedly, it has not been only the peasant girl of France, who has carried latent and hid within her person the gifts that make the supreme general. If our European nations should continue in their present semi-civilised condition, which makes war possible, for a few generations longer, it is highly probable that as financiers, as managers of the commissariat department, as inspectors of provisions and clothing for the army, women will play a very leading part; and that the nation which is the first to employ its women so may be placed at a vast advantage over its fellows in time of war. It is not because of woman's cowardice, incapacity, nor, above all, because of her general superior virtue, that she will end war when her voice is fully, finally, and clearly heard in the governance of states—it is because, on this one point, and on this point almost alone, the knowledge of woman, simply as woman, is superior to that of man; she knows the history of human flesh; she knows its cost; he does not. (It is noteworthy that even Catharine of Russia, a ruler and statesman of a virile and uncompromising type, and not usually troubled with moral scruples, yet refused with indignation the offer of Frederick of Prussia to pay her heavily for a small number of Russian recruits in an age when the hiring out of soldiers was common among the sovereigns of Europe.)

In a besieged city, it might well happen that men in the streets might seize upon statues and marble carvings from public buildings and galleries and hurl them in to stop the breaches made in their ramparts by the enemy, unconsideringly and merely because they came first to hand, not valuing them more than had they been paving-stones. But one man could not do this—the sculptor! He, who, though there might be no work of his own chisel among them, yet knew what each of these works of art had cost, knew by experience the long years of struggle and study and the infinitude of toil which had gone to the shaping of even one limb, to the carving of even one perfected outline, he could never so use them without thought or care. Instinctively he would seek to throw in household goods, even gold and silver, all the city held, before he sacrificed its works of art!

Men's bodies are our woman's works of art. Given to us power of control, we will never carelessly throw them in to fill up the gaps in human relationships made by international ambitions and greeds. The thought would never come to us as woman, "Cast in men's bodies; settle the thing so!" Arbitration and compensation would as naturally occur to her as cheaper and simpler methods of bridging the gaps in national relationships, as to the sculptor it would occur to throw in anything rather

105

than statuary, though he might be driven to that at last!

This is one of those phases of human life, not very numerous, but very important, towards which the man as man, and the woman as woman, on the mere ground of their different sexual function with regard to reproduction, stand, and must stand, at a somewhat differing angle. The physical creation of human life, which, in as far as the male is concerned, consists in a few moments of physical pleasure; to the female must always signify months of pressure and physical endurance, crowned with danger to life. To the male, the giving of life is a laugh; to the female, blood, anguish, and sometimes death. Here we touch one of the few yet important differences between man and woman as such.

The twenty thousand men prematurely slain on a field of battle, mean, to the women of their race, twenty thousand human creatures to be borne within them for months, given birth to in anguish, fed from their breasts and reared with toil, if the numbers of the tribe and the strength of the nation are to be maintained. In nations continually at war, incessant and unbroken child-bearing is by war imposed on all women if the state is to survive; and whenever war occurs, if numbers are to be maintained, there must be an increased child-bearing and rearing. This throws upon woman as woman a war tax, compared with which all that the male expends in military preparations is comparatively light.

The relations of the female towards the production of human life influences undoubtedly even her relation towards animal and all life. "It is a fine day, let us go out and kill something!" cries the typical male of certain races, instinctively. "There is a living thing, it will die if it is not cared for," says the average woman, almost equally instinctively. It is true, that the woman will sacrifice as mercilessly, as cruelly, the life of a hated rival or an enemy, as any male; but she always knows what she is doing, and the value of the life she takes! There is no light-hearted, careless enjoyment in the sacrifice of life to the normal woman;

106

her instinct, instructed by practical experience, steps in to prevent it. She always knows what life costs; and that it is more easy to destroy than create it.

It is also true, that, from the loftiest standpoint, the condemnation of war which has arisen in the advancing human spirit, is in no sense related to any particular form of sex function. The man and the woman alike, who with Isaiah on the hills of Palestine, or the Indian Buddha under his bo-tree, have seen the essential unity of all sentient life; and who therefore see in war but a symptom of that crude disco-ordination of life on earth, not yet at one with itself, which affects humanity in these early stages of its growth: and who are compelled to regard as the ultimate goal of the race, though yet perhaps far distant across the ridges of innumerable coming ages, that harmony between all forms of conscious life, metaphorically prefigured by the ancient Hebrew, when he cried, "The wolf shall dwell with the lamb; and the leopard shall lie down with the kid; and the calf and the young lion and the fatling together, and a little child shall lead them!"—to that individual, whether man or woman, who has reached this standpoint, there is no need for enlightenment from the instincts of the child-bearers of society as such; their condemnation of war, rising not so much from the fact that it is a wasteful destruction of human flesh, as that it is an indication of the non-existence of that co-ordination, the harmony which is summed up in the cry, "My little children, love one another."

But for the vast bulk of humanity, probably for generations to come, the instinctive antagonism of the human child-bearer to reckless destruction of that which she has at so much cost produced, will be necessary to educate the race to any clear conception of the bestiality and insanity of war.

War will pass when intellectual culture and activity have made possible to the female an equal share in the control and governance of modern national life; it will probably not pass away much sooner; its extinction will not be delayed much longer.

It is especially in the domain of war that we, the bearers of men's bodies, who supply its most valuable munition, who, not amid the clamour and ardour of battle, but singly, and alone, with a three-in-the-morning courage, shed our blood and face death that the battlefield may have its food, a food more precious to us than our heart's blood; it is we especially, who in the domain of war, have our word to say, a word no man can say for us. It is our intention to enter into the domain of war and to labour there till in the course of generations we have extinguished it.

If today we claim all labour for our province, yet more especially do we claim those fields in which the difference in the reproductive function between man and woman may place male and female at a slightly different angle with regard to certain phases of human life.

CHAPTER V

SEX DIFFERENCES

If we examine the physical phenomenon of sex as it manifests itself in the human creature, we find, in the first stages of the individual's existence, no difference discernible, by any means we have at present at our command, between those germs which are ultimately to become male or female. Later, in the foetal life, at birth, and through infancy though the organs of sex serve to distinguish the male from the female, there is in the general structure and working of the organism little or nothing to divide the sexes.

Even when puberty is reached, with its enormous development of sexual and reproductive activity modifying those parts of the organism with which it is concerned, and producing certain secondary sexual characteristics, there yet remains the major extent of the human body and of physical function little, or not at all, affected by sex modification. The eye, the ear, the sense of touch, the general organs of nutrition and respiration and volition are in the main identical, and often differ far more in persons of the same sex than in those of opposite sexes; and even on the dissecting-table the tissues of the male and female are often wholly indistinguishable.

It is when we consider the reproductive organs themselves and their forms of activity, and such parts of the organism modified directly in relation to them, that a real and important difference is found to exist, radical though absolutely complemental. It is exactly as we approach the reproductive functions that the male and female bodies differ; exactly as we recede from them that they become more and more similar, and even absolutely identical. Taking the eye, perhaps the most highly developed, complex organ in the body, and, if of an organ the term may be allowed, the most intellectual organ of sense, we find it remains the same in male and female in structure, in appearance, and in function throughout life; while the breast, closely connected with reproduction, though absolutely identical in both forms in infancy, assumes a widely different organisation when reproductive activity is actually concerned.

When we turn to the psychic phase of human life an exactly analogous phenomenon presents itself. The intelligence, emotions, and desires of the human infant at birth differ not at all perceptibly, as its sex may be male or female; and such psychic differences as appear to exist in later childhood are undoubtedly very largely the result of artificial training, forcing on the appearance of psychic sexual divergencies long before they would tend spontaneously to appear; as where sports and occupations are interdicted to young children on the ground of their supposed sexual unfitness; as when an infant female is forcibly prevented from climbing or shouting, and the infant male from amusing himself with needle and thread or dolls. Even in the fully adult human, and in spite of differences of training, the psychic activities over a large extent of life appear to be absolutely identical. The male and female brains acquire languages, solve mathematical problems, and master scientific detail in a manner wholly indistinguishable: as illustrated by the fact that in modern universities the papers sent in by male and female candidates are as a rule absolutely identical in type. Placed in like external conditions, their tastes and emotions, over a vast part of the surface of life, are identical; and, in an immense number of those cases where psychic sex differences appear to exist, subject to rigid analysis they are found to be purely artificial creations, for, when other races or classes are studied, they are found non-existent as sexual characteristics; as when the female is supposed by ignorant persons in modern

European societies to have an inherent love for bright colours and ornaments, not shared by the male; while experience of other societies and past social conditions prove that it is as often the male who has been even more desirous of attiring himself in bright raiment and adorning himself with brilliant jewels; or as when, among certain tribes of savages, the use of tobacco is supposed to be a peculiarly female prerogative, while, in some modern societies, it is supposed to have some relation to masculinity. (The savage male of today when attired in his paint, feathers, cats' tails and necklaces is an immeasurably more ornamented and imposing figure than his female, even when fully attired for a dance in beads and bangles: the Oriental male has sometimes scarcely been able to walk under the weight of his ornaments; and the males of Europe a couple of centuries ago, with their powdered wigs, lace ruffles and cuffs, paste buckles, feathered cocked hats, and patches were quite as ridiculous in their excess of adornment as the complementary females of their own day, or the most parasitic females of this. Both in the class and the individual, whether male or female, an intense love of dress and meretricious external adornment is almost invariably the concomitant and outcome of parasitism. Were the parasite female class in our own societies today to pass away, French fashions with their easeless and grotesque variations (shaped not for use or beauty, but the attracting of attention) would die out. And the extent to which any woman today, not herself belonging to the parasite class and still labouring, attempts to follow afar off the fashions of the parasite, may be taken generally as an almost certain indication of the ease with which she would accept parasitism were its conditions offered her. The tendency of the cultured and intellectually labouring woman of today to adopt a more rational type of attire, less shaped to attract attention to the individual than to confer comfort and abstain from impeding activity, is often spoken of as an attempt on the part of woman slavishly to imitate man. What is really taking place is, that like causes are producing like effects on

111

human creatures with common characteristics.)

But there remain certain psychic differences in attitude, on the part of male and female as such, which are inherent and not artificial: and, in the psychic human world, it is exactly as we approach the sphere of sexual and reproductive activity, with those emotions and instincts connected directly with sex and the reproduction of the race, that a difference does appear.

In the animal world all forms of psychic variations are found allying themselves now with the male sex form, and then with the female. In the insect and fish worlds, where the female forms are generally larger and stronger than the male, the female is generally more pugnacious and predatory than the male. Among birds-of-prey, where also the female form is larger and stronger than the male, the psychic differences seem very small. Among eagles and other allied forms, which are strictly monogamous, the affection of the female for the male is so great that she is said never to mate again if the male dies, and both watch over and care for the young with extreme solicitude. The ostrich male form, though perhaps larger than the female, shares with her the labour of hatching the eggs, relieving the hen of her duty at a fixed hour daily: and his care for the young when hatched is as tender as hers. Among song-birds, in which the male and female forms are so alike as sometimes to be indistinguishable, and which are also monogamous, the male and female forms not only exhibit the same passionate affection for each other (in the case of the South African cock-o-veet, they have one answering love-song between them; the male sounding two or three notes and the female completing it with two or three more), but they build the nest together and rear the young with an equal devotion. In the case of the little kapok bird of the Cape, a beautiful, white, fluffy round nest is made by both out of the white down of a certain plant, and immediately below the entrance to the cavity in which the little female sits on the eggs is a small shelf or basket, in which the tiny male sits to watch over and guard them. It is among certain orders of birds that sex manifestations appear to assume their most harmonious and poetical forms on earth. Among gallinaceous birds, on the other hand, where the cock is much larger and more pugnacious than the female, and which are polygamous, the cock does not court the female by song, but seizes her by force, and shows little or no interest in his offspring, neither sharing in the brooding nor feeding the young; and even at times seizing any tempting morsel which the young or the hen may have discovered.

Among mammals the male form tends to be slightly larger than the female, though not always (the female whale, for instance, being larger than the male); the male also tends to be more pugnacious and less careful of the young; though to this rule also there are exceptions. In the case of the South African mierkat, for instance, the female is generally more combative and more difficult to tame than the male; and it is the males who from the moment of birth watch over the young with the most passionate and tender solicitude, keeping them warm under their persons, carrying them to places of safety in their mouths, and feeding them till full grown; and this they do not only for their own young, but to any young who may be brought in contact with them. We have known a male mierkat so assiduous in feeding young that were quite unrelated to himself, taking to them every morsel of food given him, that we have been compelled to shut him up in a room alone when feeding him, to prevent his starving himself to death: the male mierkat thus exhibiting exactly those psychic qualities which are generally regarded as peculiarly feminine; the females, on the other hand, being far more pugnacious towards each other than are the males.

Among mammals generally, except the tendency to greater pugnacity shown by the male towards other males, and the greater solicitude for the young shown generally by the female form, but not always; the psychic differences between the two sex forms are not great. Between the male and female pointer as puppies, there is as little difference in mental activity as in physical; and even when adult, on the hunting ground, that great non-sexual field in which their highest mental and physical activities are displayed, there is little or nothing which distinguishes materially between the male and female; in method, manner, and quickness they are alike; in devotion to man, they are psychically identical. (It is often said the female dog is more intelligent than the male; but I am almost inclined to doubt this, after long and close study of both forms.) It is at the moment when the reproductive element comes fully into play that similarity and identity cease. In the intensity of initial sex instinct they are alike; the female will leap from windows, climb walls, and almost endanger her life to reach the male who waits for her, as readily as he will to gain her. It is when the bitch lies with her six young drawing life from her breast, and gazing with wistful and anguished solicitude at every hand stretched out to touch them, a world of emotion concentrated on the sightless creatures, and a whole body of new mental aptitudes brought into play in caring for them, it is then that between her and the male who begot them, but cares nothing for them, there does rise a psychic difference that is real and wide. Alike in the sports of puppydom and the non-sexual activities of adult age; alike in the possession of the initial sexual instinct which draws the sex to the sex, the moment active sexual reproduction is concerned, there is opened to the female a certain world of sensations and experiences, from which her male companion is for ever excluded.

So also is our human world: alike in the sports, and joys, and sorrows of infancy; alike in the non-sexual labours of life; alike even in the possession of that initial instinct which draws sex to sex, and which, differing slightly in its forms of manifestation is of corresponding intensity in both; the moment actual reproduction begins to take place, the man and the woman enter spheres of sensation, perception, emotion, desire, and knowledge which are not, and cannot be, absolutely identical. Between the man who, in an instant of light-hearted enjoyment, begets the infant (who may even beget it in a state of half-drunken unconsciousness, and may easily know nothing of its existence for months or years after it is born, or never at all; and who under no circumstances can have any direct sensational knowledge of its relation to himself) and the woman who bears it continuously for months within her body, and who gives birth to it in pain, and who, if it is to live, is compelled, or was in primitive times, to nourish it for months from the blood of her own being—between these, there exists of necessity, towards a limited but all-important body of human interests and phenomena, a certain distinct psychic attitude. At this one point, the two great halves of humanity stand confronting certain great elements in human existence, from angles that are not identical. From the moment the universal initial attraction of sex to sex becomes incarnate in the first concrete sexual act till the developed offspring attains maturity, no step in the reproductive journey, or in their relation to their offspring, has been quite identical for the man and the woman. And this divergence of experiences in human relations must react on their attitude towards that particular body of human concerns which directly is connected with the sexual reproduction of the race; and, it is exactly in these fields of human activity, where sex as sex is concerned, that woman as woman has a part to play which she cannot resign into the hands of others.

It may be truly said that in the laboratory, the designing-room, the factory, the mart, the mathematician's study, and in all fields of purely abstract or impersonal labour, while the entrance of woman would add to the net result of human labour in those fields, and though a grave injustice is done to the individual woman excluded from perhaps the only field she is fitted to excel in, that yet woman as woman has probably little or nothing to contribute in those fields that is radically distinct from that which man might supply; there would be a difference in quantity but probably none in kind, in the work done for the race.

But in those spheres of social activity, dealing especially

with certain relations between human creatures because of their diverse if complementary relation to the production of human life, the sexes as sexes have often each a part to play which the other cannot play for them; have each a knowledge gained from phases of human experience, which the other cannot supply; here woman as woman has something radically distinct to contribute to the sum-total of human knowledge, and her activity is of importance, not merely individually, but collectively, and as a class.

That demand, which today in all democratic self-governing countries is being made by women, to be accorded their share in the electoral, and ultimately in the legislative and executive duties of government, is based on two grounds: the wider, and more important, that they find nothing in the nature of their sex-function which exonerates them, as human beings, from their obligation to take part in the labours of guidance and government in their state: the narrower, but yet important ground, that, in as far as in one direction, i.e., in the special form of their sex function takes, they do differ from the male, they, in so far, form a class and are bound to represent the interests of, and to give the state the benefit of, the insight of their class, in certain directions.

Those persons who imagine that the balance of great political parties in almost any society would be seriously changed by the admission of its women in public functions are undoubtedly wholly wrong. The fundamental division of humans into those inclined to hold by the past and defend whatever is, and those hopeful of the future and inclined to introduce change, would probably be found to exist in much the same proportion were the males or the females of any given society compared: and the males and females of each class will in the main share the faults, the virtues, and the prejudices of their class. The individuals may lose by being excluded on the ground of sex from a share of public labour, and by being robbed of a portion of their lawful individual weight in their own society; and the society as a

116

whole may lose by having a smaller number to select its chosen labourers from; yet, undoubtedly, on the mass of social, political, and international questions, the conclusions arrived at by one sex would be exactly those arrived at by the other.

Were a body of humans elected to adjudicate upon Greek accents, or to pass a decision on the relative fineness of woollens and linens, the form of sex of the persons composing it would probably have no bearing on the result; there is no rational ground for supposing that, on a question of Greek accents or the thickness of cloths, equally instructed males and females would differ. Here sex plays no part. The experience and instructedness of the individuals would tell: their sexual attributes would be indifferent.

But there are points, comparatively small, even very small, in number, yet of vital importance to human life, in which sex does play a part.

It is not a matter of indifference whether the body called to adjudicate upon the questions, whether the temporary sale of the female body for sexual purposes shall or shall not be a form of traffic encouraged and recognised by the state; or whether one law shall exist for the licentious human female and another for the licentious human male; whether the claim of the female to the offspring she bears shall or shall not equal that of the male who begets it; whether an act of infidelity on the part of the male shall or shall not terminate the contract which binds his female companion to him, as completely as an act of infidelity on her part would terminate her claim on him; it is not a matter of indifference whether a body elected to adjudicate on such points as these consists of males solely, or females solely, or of both combined. As it consists of one, or the other, or of both, so not only will the answers vary, but, in some cases, will they be completely diverse. Here we come into that very narrow, but important, region, where sex as sex manifestly plays its part; where the male as male and the female as female have each their body of perceptions and experiences, which they do not hold in common; here one sex cannot adequately represent the other. It is here that each sexual part has something radically distinct to contribute to the wisdom of the race.

We, today, take all labour for our province! We seek to enter the non-sexual fields of intellectual or physical toil, because we are unable to see today, with regard to them, any dividing wall raised by sex which excludes us from them. We are yet equally determined to enter those in which sex difference does play its part, because it is here that woman, the bearer of the race, must stand side by side with man, the begetter; if a completed human wisdom, an insight that misses no aspect of human life, and an activity that is in harmony with the entire knowledge and the entire instinct of the entire human race, is to exist. It is here that the man cannot act for the woman nor the woman for the man; but both must interact. It is here that each sexual half of the race, so closely and indistinguishably blended elsewhere, has its own distinct contribution to make to the sum total of human knowledge and human wisdom. Neither is the woman without the man, nor the man without the woman, the completed human intelligence.

Therefore;—We claim, today, all labour for our province! Those large fields in which it would appear sex plays no part, and equally those smaller in which it plays a part.

CHAPTER VI

CERTAIN OBJECTIONS

It has been stated sometimes, though more often implicitly than in any direct or logical form, (this statement being one it is not easy to make definitely without its reducing itself to nullity!) that woman should seek no fields of labour in the new world of social conditions that is arising about us, as she has still her function as child-bearer: a labour which, by her own showing, is arduous and dangerous, though she may love it as a soldier loves his battlefield; and that woman should perform her sex functions only, allowing man or the state to support her, even when she is only potentially a child-bearer and bears no children. (Such a scheme, as has before been stated, was actually put forward by a literary man in England some years ago: but he had the sense to state that it should apply only to women of the upper classes, the mass of labouring women, who form the vast bulk of the English women of the present day, being left to their ill-paid drudgery and their child-bearing as well!)

There is some difficulty in replying to a theorist so wholly delusive. Not only is he to be met by all the arguments against parasitism of class or race; but, at the present day, when probably much more than half the world's most laborious and ill-paid labour is still performed by women, from tea pickers and cocoa tenders in India and the islands, to the washerwomen, cooks, and drudging labouring men's wives, who in addition to the sternest and most unending toil, throw in their child-bearing as a little addition; and when, in some civilised countries women exceed the males in numbers by one million, so that there would still be one million females for whom there was no legitimate sexual outlet, though each male in the nation supported a female, it is somewhat difficult to reply with gravity to the assertion, "Let Woman be content to be the 'Divine Child-bearer,' and ask no more."

Were it worth replying gravely to so idle a theorist, we might answer:—Through all the ages of the past, when, with heavy womb and hard labour-worn hands, we physically toiled beside man, bearing up by the labour of our bodies the world about us, it was never suggested to us, "You, the child-bearers of the race, have in that one function a labour that equals all others combined; therefore, toil no more in other directions, we pray of you; neither plant, nor build, nor bend over the grindstone; nor far into the night, while we sleep, sit weaving the clothing we and our children are to wear! Leave it to us, to plant, to reap, to weave, to work, to toil for you, O sacred child-bearer! Work no more; every man of the race will work for you!" This cry in all the grim ages of our past toil we never heard.

And today, when the lofty theorist, who tonight stands before the drawing-room fire in spotless shirtfront and perfectly fitting clothes, and declaims upon the amplitude of woman's work in life as child-bearer, and the mighty value of that labour which exceeds all other, making it unnecessary for her to share man's grosser and lower toils: is it certain he always in practical life remembers his theory? When waking tomorrow morning, he finds that the elderly house drudge, who rises at dawn while he yet sleeps to make his tea and clean his boots, has brought his tea late, and polished his boots ill; may he not even sharply condemn her, and assure her she will have to leave unless she works harder and rises earlier? Does he exclaim to her, "Divine child-bearer! Potential mother of the race! Why should you clean my boots or bring up my tea, while I lie warm in bed? Is it not enough you should have the holy and mysterious power of bringing the race to life? Let that content you. Henceforth I shall get up at dawn and make my own tea and clean my own boots, and pay you just the same!" Or, should his landlady, now about to give birth to her ninth child, send him up a poorly-cooked dinner or forget to bring up his scuttle of coals, does he send for her and thus apostrophise the astonished matron: "Child-bearer of the race! Producer of men! Cannot you be contented with so noble and lofty a function in life without toiling and moiling? Why carry up heavy coal-scuttles from the cellar and bend over hot fires, wearing out nerve and brain and muscle that should be reserved for higher duties? We, we, the men of the race, will perform its mean, its sordid, its grinding toil! For woman is beauty, peace, repose! Your function is to give life, not to support it by labour. The Mother, the Mother! How wonderful it sounds! Toil no more! Rest is for you; labour and drudgery for us!" Would he not rather assure her that, unless she laboured more assiduously and sternly, she would lose his custom and so be unable to pay her month's rent; and perhaps so, with children and an invalid or drunken husband whom she supports, be turned out into the streets? For, it is remarkable, that, with theorists of this class, it is not toil, or the amount of toil, crushing alike to brain and body, which the female undertakes that is objected to; it is the form and the amount of the reward. It is not the hand-labouring woman, even in his own society, worn out and prematurely aged at forty with grinding domestic toil, that has no beginning and knows no end—

"Man's work is from sun to sun,
But the woman's work is never done"—

it is not the haggard, work-crushed woman and mother who irons his shirts, or the potential mother who destroys health and youth in the sweater's den where she sews the garments in which he appears so radiantly in the drawing-room which disturbs him. It is the thought of the woman-doctor with an income of some hundreds a year, who drives round in her carriage to see her patients, or receives them in her consulting-rooms, and who spends the evening smoking and reading before her study fire or receiving her guests; it is the thought of the woman who, as legislator, may loll for perhaps six hours of the day on the padded seat of legislative bench, relieving the tedium now and then by a turn in the billiard- or refreshment-room, when she is not needed to vote or speak; it is the thought of the woman as Greek professor, with three or four hundred a year, who gives half a dozen lectures a week, and has leisure to enjoy the society of her husband and children, and to devote to her own study and life of thought; it is she who wrings his heart. It is not the woman, who, on hands and knees, at tenpence a day, scrubs the floors of the public buildings, or private dwellings, that fills him with anguish for womanhood: that somewhat quadrupedal posture is for him truly feminine, and does not interfere with his ideal of the mother and child-bearer; and that, in some other man's house, or perhaps his own, while he and the wife he keeps for his pleasures are visiting concert or entertainment, some weary woman paces till far into the night bearing with aching back and tired head the fretful, teething child he brought into the world, for a pittance of twenty or thirty pounds a year, does not distress him. But that the same woman by work in an office should earn one hundred and fifty pounds, be able to have a comfortable home of her own, and her evening free for study or pleasure, distresses him deeply. It is not the labour, or the amount of labour, so much as the amount of reward that interferes with his ideal of the eternal womanly; he is as a rule quite contented that the women of the race should labour for him, whether as tea-pickers or washerwomen, or toilers for the children he brings into the world, provided the reward they receive is not large, nor in such fields as he might himself at any time desire to enter.

When master and ass, drawing a heavy burden between them, have climbed a steep mountain range together; clambering over sharp rocks and across sliding gravel where no water is, and herbage is scant; if, when they were come out on the top of the mountain, and before them stretch broad, green lands, and

122

through wide half-open gates they catch the glimpse of trees waving, and there comes the sound of running waters, if then, the master should say to his ass, "Good beast of mine, lie down! I can push the whole burden myself now: lie down here; lie down, my creature; you have toiled enough; I will go on alone!" then it might be even the beast would whisper (with that glimpse through the swinging gates of the green fields beyond)—"Good master, we two have climbed this mighty mountain together, and the stones have cut my hoofs as they cut your feet. Perhaps, if when we were at the foot you had found out that the burden was two heavy for me, and had then said to me, 'Lie down, my beastie; I will carry on the burden alone; lie down and rest!' I might then have listened. But now, just here, where I see the gates swinging open, a smooth road, and green fields before us, I think I shall go on a little farther. We two have climbed together; maybe we shall go on yet, side by side."

For the heart of labouring womanhood cries out today to the man who would suggest she need not seek new fields of labour, that child-bearing is enough for her share in life's labour, "Do you dare say to us now, that we are fit to do nothing but child-bear, that when that is performed our powers are exhausted? To us, who yet through all the ages of the past, when child-bearing was persistent and incessant, regarded it hardly as a toil, but rather as the reward of labour; has our right hand lost its cunning and our heart its strength, that today, when human labour is easier and humanity's work grows fairer, you say to us, 'You can do nothing now but child-bear'? Do you dare to say this, to us, when the upward path of the race has been watered by the sweat of our brow, and the sides of the road by which humanity has climbed are whitened on either hand by the bones of the womanhood that has fallen there, toiling beside man? Do you dare say this, to us, when even today the food you eat, the clothes you wear, the comfort you enjoy, is largely given you by the unending muscular toil of woman?"

As the women of old planted and reaped and ground the

grain that the children they bore might eat; as the maidens of old spun that they might make linen for their households and obtain the right to bear men; so, though we bend no more over grindstones, or labour in the fields, or weave by hand, it is our intention to enter all the new fields of labour, that we also may have the power and right to bring men into the world. It is our faith that the day comes in which not only shall no man dare to say, "It is enough portion for a woman in life that she bear a child," but when it will rather be said, "What noble labour has that woman performed, that she should have the privilege of bringing a man or woman child into the world?"

But, it has also been objected, "What, and if the female half of humanity, though able, in addition to the exercise of its reproductive functions, to bear its share in the new fields of social labour as it did in the old, be yet in certain directions a less productive labourer than the male? What if, in the main, the result of the labour of the two halves of humanity should not be found to be exactly equal?"

To this it may be answered, that it is within the range of possibility that, mysteriously co-ordinated with the male reproductive function in the human, there may also be in some directions a tendency to possess gifts for labour useful and beneficial to the race in the stage of growth it has now reached, in excess of those possessed by the female. We see no reason why this should be so, and, in the present state of our knowledge, this is a point on which no sane person would dogmatise; but it is possible! It may, on the other hand be, that, taken in the bulk, when all the branches of productive labour be considered, as the ages pass, the value of the labour of the two halves of humanity will be found so identical and so closely to balance, that no superiority can possibly be asserted of either, as the result of the closest analysis. This also is possible.

But, it may also be, that, when the bulk and sum-total of human activities is surveyed in future ages, it will be found that the value of the labour of the female in the world that is rising about us, has exceeded in quality or in quantity that of the male. We see no reason either, why this should be; there is nothing in the nature of the reproductive function in the female human which of necessity implies such superiority.

Yet it may be, that, with the smaller general bulk and the muscular fineness, and the preponderance of brain and nervous system in net bulk over the fleshy and osseous parts of the organism, which generally, though by no means always, characterises the female as distinguished from the male of the human species, there do go mental qualities which will peculiarly fit her for the labours of the future. It may be, that her lesser possession of the mere muscular and osseous strength, which were the elements of primary importance and which gave dominance in one stage of human growth, and which placed woman at a social disadvantage as compared with her companion, will, under new conditions of life, in which the value of crude mechanical strength as distinguished from high vitality and strong nervous activity is passing away, prove as largely to her advantage, as his muscular bulk and strength in the past proved to the male. It is quite possible, in the new world which is arising about us, that the type of human most useful to society and best fitted for its future conditions, and who will excel in the most numerous forms of activity, will be, not merely the muscularly powerful and bulky, but the highly versatile, active, vital, adaptive, sensitive, physically fine-drawn type; and, as that type, though, like the muscularly heavy and powerful, by no means peculiar to and confined to one sex, is yet rather more commonly found in conjunction with a female organism, it is quite possible that, taken in the bulk and on the whole, the female half of humanity may, by virtue of its structural adaptions, be found most fitted for the bulk of human labours in the future!

As with individuals and races, so also with sexes, changed social conditions may render exactly those subtile qualities, which in one social state were a disadvantage, of the highest social advantage in another.

The skilled diplomatist or politician, so powerful in his own element, on board ship during a storm becomes at once of less general value or consideration than the meanest sailor who can reef a sail or guide a wheel; and, were we to be reduced again suddenly to a state of nature, a company of highly civilised men and women would at once, as we have before remarked, find their social value completely inverted; landed on a desert shore, unarmed and naked, to encounter wild beasts and savages, and to combat nature for food, the primitive scale of human values would at once reassert itself. It would not then be the mighty financier, the learned judge, or great poet and scholar who would be sought after, but the thickest-headed navvy who could throw a stone so exactly that he brought down a bird, and who could in a day raise a wall which would shelter the group; and the man so powerful that he could surely strike an enemy or wild beast dead with his club, would at once be objects of social regard and attain individual eminence, and perhaps dominance. It would not be the skilled dancer, who in one night in a civilised state earns her hundreds, nor yet the fragile clinging beauty, but the girl of the broad back and the strong limb, who could collect wood and carry water, who would be the much considered and much sought after female in such a community. Even in the animal world, there is the same inversion in values, according as the external conditions vary. The lion, while ruling over every other creature in his primitive wilds, by right of his untamable ferocity, size, and rapacity, is yet bound to become a prey to destruction and extermination when he comes into contact with the new condition brought by man; while the wild dog, so immeasurably his inferior in size and ferocity, is tamed, survives and multiplies, exactly because he has been driven by his smaller structure and lesser physical force to develop those social instincts and those forms of intelligence which make him amenable to the new condition of life and valuable in them. The same inversion in the value of qualities may be traced in the history of human species. The Jews, whose history has been one long story of oppression at the hands of more muscular, physically powerful and pugilistic peoples; whom we find first making bricks under the lash of the Egyptian, and later hanging his harp as an exile among the willow-trees of Babylon; who, for eighteen hundred years, has been trampled, tortured, and despised beneath the feet of the more physically powerful and pugilistic, but not more vital, keen, intelligent, or persistent races of Europe; has, today, by the slow turning of the wheel of life, come uppermost. The Egyptian task-master and warrior have passed; what the Babylonian was we know no more, save for a few mud tablets and rock inscriptions recording the martial victories; but the once captive Jew we see today in every city and every street; until at last, the descendants of those men who spat when they spoke his name, and forcibly drew his teeth to extract his money from him, wait patiently behind each other for admission to his offices and palaces; while nobles solicit his daughters in marriage and kings are proud to be summoned to his table in hope of golden crumbs, and great questions of peace and war are often held balanced in the hand of one little asthmatic Jew. After long ages of disgrace and pariahism, the time has come, whether for good or for evil, when just those qualities which the Jew possesses and which subtilely distinguish him from others, are in demand; while those he has not are sinking into disuse; exactly that domination of the reflective faculties over the combative, which once made him slave, also saved him from becoming extinct in wars; and the intellectual quickness, the far-sighted keenness, the persistent mental activity and self-control, which could not in those ages save him from degradation or compensate for his lack of bone and muscle and combative instinct, are the very qualities the modern world demands and crowns. The day of Goliath with his club and his oaths is fast passing, and the day of David with his harp and skilfully constructed sling is coming near and yet nearer.

The qualities which give an animal, a race, or an individual, a higher utility or social dominance must always be influenced by any change in the environment. As the wheel of life slowly revolves, that which was lowest comes continually uppermost, and that which was dominant becomes subservient.

It is possible, that women, after countless ages, during which that smaller relative development in weight and muscularity which is incident to almost all females which suckle their young, and that lesser desire for pugilism inherent in almost all females who bear their young alive, rendered her lacking in the two qualities which made for individual dominance in her societies, may yet, in the future, discover that those changes in human conditions, which have done away with the primary necessity for muscular force and pugilistic arts, have also inverted her place in the scale of social values.

It is possible, that the human female, like the Jew, the male of that type farthest removed from the dominant male type of the past, may in the future find, that, so far from those qualities which, in an earlier condition, lessened her social value and power of labour, continuing to do so, they will increase it. That the delicacy of hand, lightness of structure which were fatal when the dominant labour of life was to wield a battle-axe or move a weight, may be no restraint but even an assistance in the intellectual and more delicate mechanical fields of labour; that the preponderance of nervous and cerebral over muscular material, and the tendency towards preservative and creative activity over pugilistic and destructive, so far from shutting her off from the most important fields of human toil, may increase her fitness for them! We have no certain proof that it is so at present; but, if woman's long years of servitude and physical subjection, and her experience as child-bearer and protector of infancy, should, in any way, be found in the future to have endowed her, as a kind of secondary sexual characteristic, with any additional strength of social instinct, with any exceptional width of human sympathy and any instinctive comprehension; then, it is not merely possible, but certain, that, in the ages that are coming, in which the labour of the human race will be not mainly destructive but conservative, in which the building up and developing of humanity, and not continually the inter-destruction of part by part, will be the dominant activity of the race, that woman as woman, and by right of that wherein she differs from the male, will have an all-important part to play in the activity of the race.

The matter is one of curious and subtle interest, but what practically concerns the human race is, not which of the two sexual halves which must always coexist is best fitted to excel in certain human labours in this or that direction, at this or that time, nor even which has most to contribute to the sum-total of human activities; but it is this, that every individual unit humanity contains, irrespective of race, sex, or type, should find exactly that field of labour which may most contribute to its development, happiness, and health, and in which its peculiar faculties and gifts shall be most effectively and beneficially exerted for its fellows.

It matters nothing, and less than nothing, to us as women, whether, of those children we bring into the world, our sons should excel in virtue, intelligence, and activity, our daughters, or our daughters our sons; so that, in each child we bring to life, not one potentiality shall be lost, nor squandered on a lesser when it might have been expended on a higher and more beneficent task. So that not one desirable faculty of the marvellous creatures we suffer to bring into existence be left uncultivated, to us, as women, it matters nothing and less than nothing, which sex type excels in action, in knowledge, or in virtue, so both attain their best. There is one thing only on earth, as precious to woman as the daughter who springs from her body—it is the son. There is one thing only dearer to the woman than herself—it is the man. As no sane human concerns himself as to whether the right or left ventricle of his heart works most satisfactorily, or is most essential to his well-being, so both be perfect in health and activity; as no sane woman distresses herself lest her right breast should not excel the left in beauty and use; so no sane man or woman questions anxiously over the relative perfections of male and female. In love there is no first nor last. What we request of life is that the tools should be given to his hand or hers who can best handle them; that the least efficient should not be forced into the place of the more efficient, and that an artificially drawn line should never repress the activities of the individual creature, which we as women bring into the world.

But it may also be said to us, "What, and if, all your dreams and hopes for woman and the future of the race be based on air? What, and if, desirable as it is that woman should not become practically dependent on her sexual function alone, and should play at least as great a part in the productive labour of the race in the future as she played in that of the past—what, if woman cannot take the same vast share in the complex and largely mental labour fields of the future, as in the largely physical fields of the past? What, and if, in spite of all her effort and sacrifice to attain this end, exactly now and when the labour of civilised societies becomes mental rather than mechanical, woman be found wanting?"

In Swiss valleys today the traveller comes sometimes on the figure of a solitary woman climbing the mountain-side, on her broad shoulders a mighty burden of fodder or manure she is bearing up for the cattle, or to some patch of cultivated land. Steady, unshrinking eyes look out at you from beneath the deeply seamed forehead, and a strand of hair, perhaps almost as white as the mountain snows on the peaks above, escapes from under the edge of the binding handkerchief. The face is seamed and seared with the stern marks of toil and endurance, as the mountain-side is with marks of storm and avalanche. It is the face of one who has brought men into the world in labour and sorrow, and toiled mightily to sustain them; and dead must be the mind to the phases of human existence, who does not see in that toilworn figure one of the mighty pillars, which have in the long ages of the past sustained the life of humanity on earth, and made possible its later development; and much must the tinsel of life have dazzled him, who fails to mark it with reverence and, metaphorically, to bow his head before it—the type of the mighty labouring woman who has built up life.

But, it may be said, what if, in the ages to come, it should never again be possible for any man to stand bowed with the same respect in the presence of any other of earth's mighty toilers, who should also be mother and woman? What, if she, who could combine motherhood with the most unending muscular toil, will fall flaccid and helpless where the labour becomes mental? What if, struggle as she will, she can become nothing in the future but the pet pug-dog of the race, lying on its sofa, or the Italian greyhound, shivering in its silken coat? What if woman, in spite of her most earnest aspirations and determined struggles, be destined to failure in the new world that is rising because of inherent mental incapacity?

There are many replies which may be made to such a suggestion. It is often said with truth, that the ordinary occupations of woman in the past and present, and in all classes of society in which she is not parasitic, do demand, and have always demanded, a very high versatility and mental activity, as well as physical: that the mediaeval baron's wife who guided her large household probably had to expend far more pure intellect in doing so than the baron in his hunting and fighting; that the wife of the city accountant probably expends today more reason, imagination, forethought, and memory on the management of her small household, than he in his far simpler, monotonous arithmetical toil; that, as there is no cause for supposing that the tailor or shoemaker needs less intellect in his calling than the soldier or prize-fighter, so there is nothing to suggest that, in the past, woman has not expended as much pure intellect in the mass of her callings as the man in his; while in those highly specialised intellectual occupations, in which long and uninterrupted training tending to one point is necessary, such as the liberal professions and arts, that, although woman has

131

practically been excluded from the requisite training, and the freedom to place herself in the positions in which they can be pursued, that yet, by force of innate genius and gifts in such directions, she has continually broken through the seemingly insuperable obstacles, and again and again taken her place beside man in those fields of labour; showing thereby not merely aptitude but passionate and determined inclination in those directions. With equal truth, it is often remarked that, when as an independent hereditary sovereign, woman has been placed in the only position in which she has ever been able freely and fully to express her own individuality, and though selected at random by fate from the mass of women, by the mere accident of birth or marriage, she has shown in a large percentage of cases that the female has the power to command, organise, and succeed in one of the most exacting and complex of human employments, the government of nations; that from the days of Amalasontha to Isabella of Spain, Elizabeth of England, and Catharine of Russia, women have not failed to grasp the large impersonal aspects of life, and successfully and powerfully to control them, when placed in the supreme position in which it was demanded. It may also be stated, and is sometimes, with so much iteration as to become almost wearisome, that women's adequacy in the modern fields of intellectual or skilled manual labour is no more today an open matter for debate, than the number of modern women who, as senior wranglers, doctors, &c., have already successfully entered the new fields, and the high standard attained by women in all university examinations to which they are admitted, and their universal success in the administration of parochial matters, wherever they have been allowed to share it, proves their intellectual and moral fitness for the new forms of labour.

All these statements are certainly interesting, and may be unanswerable. And yet—if the truth be told, it is not ultimately on these grounds that many of us base our hope and our certitude with regard to the future of woman. Our conviction as to the plenitude of her powers for the adequate performance of lofty labours in these new fields, springs not at all from a categorical enumeration of the attainments or performances of individual women or bodies of women in the past or present; it has another source.

There was a bird's egg once, picked up by chance upon the ground, and those who found it bore it home and placed it under a barn-door fowl. And in time the chick bred out, and those who had found it chained it by the leg to a log, lest it should stray and be lost. And by and by they gathered round it, and speculated as to what the bird might be. One said, "It is surely a waterfowl, a duck, or it may be a goose; if we took it to the water it would swim and gabble." But another said, "It has no webs to its feet; it is a barn-door fowl; should you let it loose it will scratch and cackle with the others on the dung-heap." But a third speculated, "Look now at its curved beak; no doubt it is a parrot, and can crack nuts!" But a fourth said, "No, but look at its wings; perhaps it is a bird of great flight." But several cried, "Nonsense! No one has ever seen it fly! Why should it fly? Can you suppose that a thing can do a thing which no one has ever seen it do?" And the bird—the bird—with its leg chained close to the log, preened its wing. So they sat about it, speculating, and discussing it: and one said this, and another that. And all the while as they talked the bird sat motionless, with its gaze fixed on the clear, blue sky above it. And one said, "Suppose we let the creature loose to see what it will do?"—and the bird shivered. But the others cried, "It is too valuable; it might get lost. If it were to try to fly it might fall down and break its neck." And the bird, with its foot chained to the log, sat looking upward into the clear blue sky; the sky, in which it had never been—for the bird—the bird, knew what it would do—because it was an eaglet!

There is one woman known to many of us, as each human creature knows but one on earth; and it is upon our knowledge of that woman that we base our certitude.

For those who do not know her, and have not this ground, it

is probably profitable and necessary that they painfully collect isolated facts and then speculate upon them, and base whatever views they should form upon these collections. It might even be profitable that they should form no definite opinions at all, but wait till the ages of practical experience have put doubt to rest. For those of us who have a ground of knowledge which we cannot transmit to outsiders, it is perhaps more profitable to act fearlessly than to argue.

Finally, it may be objected to the entrance of woman to the new fields of labour, and in effect it is often said—"What, and if, all you have sought be granted you—if it be fully agreed that woman's ancient fields of toil are slipping from her, and that, if she do not find new, she must fall into a state of sexual parasitism, dependent on her reproductive functions alone; and granted, that, doing this, she must degenerate, and that from her degeneration must arise the degeneration and arrest of development of the males as well as of the females of her race; and granting also, fully, that in the past woman has borne one full half, and often more than one half, of the weight of the productive labours of her societies, in addition to childbearing; and allowing more fully that she may be as well able to sustain her share in the intellectual labours of the future as in the more mechanical labours of the past; granting all this, may there not be one aspect of the question left out of consideration which may reverse all conclusions as to the desirability, and the human good to be attained by woman's enlarged freedom and her entering into the new fields of toil? What if, the increased culture and mental activity of woman necessary for her entrance into the new fields, however desirable in other ways for herself and the race, should result in a diminution, or in an absolute abolition of the sexual attraction and affection, which in all ages of the past has bound the two halves of humanity together? What if, though the stern and unlovely manual labours of the past have never affected her attractiveness for the male of her own society, nor his for her; yet the performance by woman of intellectual labours, or complex and interesting manual labour, and her increased intelligence and width, should render the male objectionable to her, and the woman undesirable to the male; so that the very race itself might become extinct through the dearth of sexual affection? What, and if, the woman ceases to value the son she bears, and to feel desire for and tenderness to the man who begets him; and the man to value and desire the woman and her offspring? Would not such a result exceed, or at least equal, in its evil to humanity, anything which could result from the degeneration and parasitism of woman? Would it not be well, if there exist any possibility of this danger, that woman, however conscious that she can perform social labour as nobly and successfully under the new conditions of life as the old, should yet consciously, and deliberately, with her eyes open, sink into a state of pure intellectual torpor, with all its attendant evils, rather than face the more irreparable loss which her development and the exercise of her gifts might entail? Would it not be well she should deliberately determine, as the lesser of two evils, to dwarf herself and limit her activities and the expansion of her faculties, rather than that any risk should be run of the bond of desire and emotion between the two sexual halves of humanity being severed? If the race is to decay and become extinct on earth, might it not as well be through the parasitism and decay of woman, as through the decay of the sexual instinct?"

It is not easy to reply with rationality, or even gravity, to a supposition, which appears to be based on the conception that a sudden and entire subversion of the deepest of those elements on which human, and even animal, life on the globe is based, is possible from so inadequate a cause: and it might well be passed silently, were it not that, under some form or other, this argument frequently recurs, now in a more rational and then in a more irrational form; constituting sometimes an objection in even moderately intelligent minds, to the entrance of woman into the new fields of labour.

It must be at once frankly admitted that, were there the smallest possible danger in this direction, the sooner woman laid aside all endeavour in the direction of increased knowledge and the attainment of new fields of activity, the better for herself and for the race.

When one considers the part which sexual attraction plays in the order of sentient life on the globe, from the almost unconscious attractions which draw amoeboid globule to amoeboid globule, on through the endless progressive forms of life; till in monogamous birds it expresses itself in song and complex courtship and sometimes in the life-long conjugal affection of mates; and which in the human race itself, passing through various forms, from the imperative but almost purely physical attraction of savage male and female for each other, till in the highly developed male and female it assumes its aesthetic and intellectual but not less imperative form, couching itself in the songs of poet, and the sometimes deathless fidelity of richly developed man and woman to each other, we find it not only everywhere, but forming the very groundwork on which is based sentient existence; never eradicable, though infinitely varied in its external forms of expression. When we consider that in the human world, from the battles and dances of savages to the intrigues and entertainments of modern Courts and palaces, the attraction of man and woman for each other has played an unending part; and, that the most fierce ascetic religious enthusiasm through the ages, the flagellations and starvations in endless nunneries and monasteries, have never been able to extirpate nor seriously to weaken for one moment the master dominance of this emotion; that the lowest and most brutal ignorance, and the highest intellectual culture leave mankind, equally, though in different forms, amenable to its mastery; that, whether in the brutal guffaw of sex laughter which rings across the drinking bars of our modern cities, and rises from the comfortable armchairs in fashionable clubs; or in the poet's dreams, and the noblest conjugal relations of men and women linked together for life, it plays still today on earth the vast part it played when hoary monsters ploughed after each other through Silurian slime, and that still it forms as ever the warp on which in the loom of human life the web is woven, and runs as a thread never absent through every design and pattern which constitutes the individual existence on earth, it appears not merely as ineradicable; but it is inconceivable to suppose that that attraction of sex towards sex, which, with hunger and thirst, lie, as the triune instincts, at the base of animal life on earth, should ever be exterminable by the comparatively superficial changes resulting from the performance of this or that form of labour, or the little more or less of knowledge in one direction or another.

That the female who drives steam-driven looms, producing scores of yards of linen in a day, should therefore desire less the fellowship of her corresponding male than had she toiled at a spinning-wheel with hand and foot to produce one yard; that the male should desire less of the companionship of the woman who spends the morning in doctoring babies in her consulting-room, according to the formularies of the pharmacopoeia, than she who of old spent it on the hillside collecting simples for remedies; that the woman who paints a modern picture or designs a modern vase should be less lovable by man, than her ancestor who shaped the first primitive pot and ornamented it with zigzag patterns was to the man of her day and age; that the woman who contributes to the support of her family by giving legal opinions will less desire motherhood and wifehood than she who in the past contributed to the support of her household by bending on hands and knees over her grindstone, or scrubbing floors, and that the former should be less valued by man than the latter—these are suppositions which it is difficult to regard as consonant with any knowledge of human nature and the laws by which it is dominated.

On the other hand, if it be supposed that the possession of wealth or the means of earning it makes the human female objectionable to the male, all history and all daily experience negates it. The eager hunt for heiresses in all ages and social conditions, make it obvious that the human male has a strong tendency to value the female who can contribute to the family expenditure; and the case is yet, we believe, unrecorded of a male who, attracted to a female, becomes averse to her on finding she has material good. The female doctor or lawyer earning a thousand a year will always, and today certainly does, find more suitors than had she remained a governess or cook, labouring as hard, earning thirty pounds.

While, if the statement that the female entering on new fields of labour will cease to be lovable to the male be based on the fact that she will then be free, all history and all human experience yet more negates its truth. The study of all races in all ages, proves that the greater the freedom of woman in any society, the higher the sexual value put upon her by the males of that society. The three squaws who walk behind the Indian, and whom he has captured in battle or bought for a few axes or lengths of tobacco, and over whom he exercises the despotic right of life and death, are probably all three of infinitesimal value in his eyes, compared with the value of his single, free wife to one of our ancient, monogamous German ancestors; while the hundred wives and concubines purchased by a Turkish pasha have probably not even an approximate value in his eyes, when compared with the value which thousands of modern European males set upon the one comparatively free woman, whom they may have won, often only after a long and tedious courtship.

So axiomatic is the statement that the value of the female to the male varies as her freedom, that, given an account of any human society in which the individual female is highly valued, it will be perfectly safe to infer the comparative social freedom of woman; and, given a statement as to the high degree of freedom of woman in a society, it will be safe to infer the great sexual value of the individual woman to man.

Finally, if the suggestion, that men and women will cease

to be attractive to one another if women enter modern fields of labour, be based on the fact that her doing so may increase her intelligence and enlarge her intellectual horizon, it must be replied that the whole trend of human history absolutely negates the supposition. There is absolutely no ground for the assumption that increased intelligence and intellectual power diminishes sexual emotion in the human creature of either sex. The ignorant savage, whether in ancient or modern societies, who violates and then clubs a female into submission, may be dominated, and is, by sex emotions of a certain class; but not less dominated have been the most cultured, powerful, and highly differentiated male intelligences that the race has produced. A Mill, a Shelley, a Goethe, a Schiller, a Pericles, have not been more noted for vast intellectual powers, than for the depth and intensity of their sexual emotions. And, if possible, with the human female, the relation between intensity of sexual emotion and high intellectual gifts has been yet closer. The life of a Sophia Kovalevsky, a George Eliot, an Elizabeth Browning have not been more marked by a rare development of the intellect than by deep passionate sexual emotions. Nor throughout the history of the race has high intelligence and intellectual power ever tended to make either male or female unattractive to those of the opposite sex.

The merely brilliantly attired and unintelligent woman, probably never awakened the same intensity of profound sex emotion even among the men of her own type, which followed a George Sand; who attracted to herself with deathless force some of the most noted men of her generation, even when, nearing middle age, stout, and attired in rusty and inartistic black, she was to be found rolling her cigarettes in a dingy office, scorning all the external adornments with which less attractive females seek to supply a hidden deficiency. Probably no more hopeless mistake could be made by an ascetic seeking to extirpate sex emotion and the attraction of the sexes for one another, than were he to imagine that in increasing virility, intelligence, and knowledge this end could be attained. He might thereby differentiate and greatly concentrate the emotions, but they would be intensified; as a widely spread, shallow, sluggish stream would not be annihilated but increased in force and activity by being turned into a sharply defined, clear-cut course.

And if, further, we turn to those secondary manifestations of sexual emotion, which express themselves in the relations of human progenitors to their offspring, we shall find, if possible more markedly, that increase of intelligence and virility does not diminish but increases the strength of the affections. As the primitive, ignorant male, often willingly selling his offspring or exposing his female infants to death, often develops, with the increase of culture and intelligence, into the extremely devoted and self-sacrificing male progenitor of civilised societies; so, yet even more markedly, does the female relation with her offspring, become intensified and permanent, as culture and intelligence and virility increase. The Bushwoman, like the lowest female barbarians in our own societies, will often readily dispose of her infant son for a bottle of spirits or a little coin; and even among somewhat more mentally developed females, strong as is the affection of the average female for her new born offspring, the closeness of the relation between mother and child tends rapidly to shrink as time passes, so that by the time of adolescence is reached the relation between mother and son becomes little more than a remembrance of a close inter-union which once existed. It is, perhaps, seldom, till the very highest point of intellectual growth and mental virility has been reached by the human female, that her relation with her male offspring becomes a permanent and active and dominant factor in the lives of both. The concentrated and all-absorbing affection and fellowship which existed between the greatest female intellect France has produced and the son she bore, dominating both lives to the end, the fellowship of the English historian with his mother, who remained his chosen companion and the sharer of all his labours through life, the relation of St. Augustine to his mother, and those of countless others, are relations almost inconceivable where the woman is not of commanding and active intelligence, and where the passion of mere physical instinct is completed by the passion of the intellect and spirit.

There appears, then, from the study of human nature in the past, no ground for supposing that if, as a result of woman's adopting new forms of labour, she should become more free, more wealthy, or more actively intelligent, that this could in any way diminish her need of the physical and mental comradeship of man, nor his need of her; nor that it would affect their secondary sexual relations as progenitors, save by deepening, concentrating, and extending throughout life the parental emotions. The conception that man's and woman's need of each other could be touched, or the emotions binding the sexes obliterated, by any mere change in the form of labour performed by the woman of the race, is as grotesque in its impossibility, as the suggestion that the placing of a shell on the seashore this way or that might destroy the action of the earth's great tidal wave.

But, it may be objected, "If there be absolutely no ground for the formation of such an opinion, how comes it that, in one form or another, it is so often expressed by persons who object to the entrance of woman into new or intellectual fields of labour? Where there is smoke must there not also be fire?" To which it must be replied, "Without fire, no smoke; but very often the appearance of smoke where neither smoke nor fire exist!"

The fact that a statement is frequently made or a view held forms no presumptive ground of its truth; but it is undoubtedly a ground for supposing that there is an appearance or semblance which makes it appear truth, and which suggests it. The universally entertained conception that the sun moved round the world was not merely false, but the reverse of the truth; all that was required for its inception was a fallacious appearance suggesting it.

When we examine narrowly the statement, that the entrance of woman into the new fields of labour, with its probably resulting greater freedom of action, economic independence and wider culture, may result in a severance between the sexes, it becomes clear what that fallacious appearance is, which suggests this.

The entrance of a woman into new fields of labour, though bringing her increased freedom and economic independence, and necessitating increased mental training and wider knowledge, could not extinguish the primordial physical instinct which draws sex to sex throughout all the orders of sentient life; and still less could it annihilate that subtler mental need, which, as humanity develops, draws sex to sex for emotional fellowship and close intercourse; but, it might, and undoubtedly would, powerfully react and readjust the relations of certain men with certain women!

While the attraction, physical and intellectual, which binds sex to sex would remain the same in volume and intensity, the forms in which it would express itself, and, above all, the relative power of individuals to command the gratification of their instincts and desires, would be fundamentally altered, and in many cases inverted.

In the barbarian state of societies, where physical force dominates, it is the most muscular and pugilistically and brutally and animally successful male who captures and possesses the largest number of females; and no doubt he would be justified in regarding any social change which gave to woman a larger freedom of choice, and which would so perhaps give to the less brutal but perhaps more intelligent male, whom the woman might select, an equal opportunity for the gratification of his sexual wishes and for the producing of offspring, as a serious loss. And, from the purely personal standpoint, he would undoubtedly be right in dreading anything which tended to free woman. But he would manifestly not have been justified in asserting, that woman's increased freedom of choice, or the fact that the other men would share his advantage in the matter of obtaining female companionship, would in any way lessen the amount of sexual emotion or the tenderness of relation between the two halves of humanity. He would not by brute force possess himself of so many females, nor have so large a circle of choice, under the new conditions; but what he lost, others would gain; and the intensity of the sex emotions and the nearness and passion of the relation between the sexes be in no way touched.

In our more civilised societies, as they exist today, woman possesses (more often perhaps in appearance than reality!) a somewhat greater freedom of sexual selection; she is no longer captured by muscular force, but there are still conditions entirely unconnected with sex attractions and affections, which yet largely dominate the sex relations.

It is not the man of the strong arm, but the man of the long purse, who unduly and artificially dominates in the sexual world today. Practically, wherever in the modern world woman is wholly or partially dependent for her means of support on the exercise of her sexual functions, she is dependent more or less on the male's power to support her in their exercise, and her freedom of choice is practically so far absolutely limited. Probably three-fourths of the sexual unions in our modern European societies, whether in the illegal or recognised legal forms, are dominated by or largely influenced by the sex purchasing power of the male. With regard to the large and savage institution of prostitution, which still lies as the cancer embedded in the heart of all our modern civilised societies, this is obviously and nakedly the case; the wealth of the male as compared to the female being, with hideous obtrusiveness, its foundation and source of life. But the purchasing power of the male as compared with the poverty of the female is not less painfully, if a little less obtrusively, displayed in those layers of society lying nearer the surface. From the fair, effete young girl of the wealthier classes in her city boudoir, who weeps copiously as she tells you she cannot marry the man she loves, because he says he has only two hundred a year and cannot afford to keep her; to the father who demands frankly of his daughter's suitor how much he can settle on her before consenting to his acceptance, the fact remains, that, under existing conditions, not the amount of sex affection, passion, and attraction, but the extraneous question of the material possessions of the male, determines to a large extent the relation of the sexes. The parasitic, helpless youth who has failed in his studies, who possesses neither virility, nor charm of person, nor strength of mind, but who possesses wealth, has a far greater chance of securing unlimited sexual indulgence and the life companionship of the fairest maid, than her brother's tutor, who may be possessed of every manly and physical grace and mental gift; and the ancient libertine, possessed of nothing but material good, has, especially among the so-called upper classes of our societies, a far greater chance of securing the sex companionship of any woman he desires as wife, mistress, or prostitute, than the most physically attractive and mentally developed male, who may have nothing to offer to the dependent female but affection and sexual companionship.

To the male, whenever and wherever he exists in our societies, who depends mainly for his power for procuring the sex relation he desires, not on his power of winning and retaining personal affection, but, on the purchasing power of his possessions as compared to the poverty of the females of his society, the personal loss would be seriously and at once felt, of any social change which gave to the woman a larger economic independence and therefore greater freedom of sexual choice. It is not an imaginary danger which the young dude, of a certain type which sits often in the front row of the stalls in a theatre, with sloping forehead and feeble jaw, watching the unhappy women who dance for gold—sees looming before him, as he lisps out his deep disapproval of increased knowledge and the freedom of obtaining the means of subsistence in intellectual fields by woman, and expresses his vast preference for the uncultured ballet-girl over all types of cultured and productive labouring womenhood in the universe. A subtle and profound instinct warns him, that with the increased intelligence and economic freedom of woman, he, and such as he, might ultimately be left sexually companionless; the undesirable, the residuary, male old-maids of the human race.

On the other hand, there is undoubtedly a certain body of females who would lose, or imagine they would lose, heavily by the advance of woman as a whole to a condition of free labour and economic independence. That female, wilfully or organically belonging to the parasite class, having neither the vigour of intellect nor the vitality of body to undertake any form of productive labour, and desiring to be dependent only upon the passive performance of sex function merely, would, whether as prostitute or wife, undoubtedly lose heavily by any social change which demanded of woman increased knowledge and activity. (She would lose in two directions: by the social disapprobation which, as the new conditions became general, would rest on her; and yet more by the competition of the more developed forms. She would practically become non-existent.)

It is exactly by these two classes of persons that the objection is raised that the entrance of woman into the new fields of labour and her increased freedom and intelligence will dislocate the relations of the sexes; and, while from the purely personal standpoint, they are undoubtedly right, viewing human society as a whole they are fundamentally wrong. The loss of a small and unhealthy section will be the gain of human society as a whole.

In the male voluptuary of feeble intellect and unattractive individuality, who depends for the gratification of his sexual instincts, not on his power of winning and retaining the personal affection and admiration of woman, but on her purchaseable condition, either in the blatantly barbarous field of sex traffic that lies beyond the pale of legal marriage, or the not less barbarous though more veiled traffic within that pale, the entrance of woman into the new fields of labour, with an increased intellectual culture and economic freedom, means little less than social extinction. But, to those males who, even at the present day, constitute the majority in our societies, and who desire the affection and fellowship of woman rather than a mere material possession; for the male who has the attributes and gifts of mind or body, which, apart from any weight of material advantage, would fit him to hold the affection of woman, however great her freedom of choice, the gain will be correspondingly great. Given a society in which the majority of women should be so far self-supporting, that, having their free share open to them in the modern fields of labour, and reaping the full economic rewards of their labour, marriage or some form of sexual sale was no more a matter of necessity to them; so far from this condition causing a diminution in the number of permanent sex unions, one of the heaviest bars to them would be removed. It is universally allowed that one of the disease spots in our modern social condition is the increasing difficulty which bars conscientious men from entering on marriage and rearing families, if limited means would in the case of their death or disablement throw the woman and their common offspring comparatively helpless into the fierce stream of our modern economic life. If the woman could justifiably be looked to, in case of the man's disablement or death, to take his place as an earner, thousands of valuable marriages which cannot now be contracted could be entered on; and the serious social evil, which arises from the fact that while the self-indulgent and selfish freely marry and produce large families, the restrained and conscientious are often unable to do so, would be removed. For the first time in the history of the modern world, prostitution, using that term in its broadest sense to cover all forced sexual relationships based, not on the spontaneous affection of the woman for the man, but on the necessitous acceptance by woman of material good in exchange for the exercise of her sexual functions, would be extinct; and the relation between men and women become a co-partnership between freemen.

So far from the economic freedom and social independence of the woman exterminating sexual love between man and woman, it would for the first time fully enfranchise it. The element of physical force and capture which dominated the most primitive sex relations, the more degrading element of seduction and purchase by means of wealth or material good offered to woman in our modern societies, would then give place to the untrammelled action of attraction and affection alone between the sexes, and sexual love, after its long pilgrimage in the deserts, would be enabled to return at last, a king crowned.

But, apart from the two classes of persons whose objection to the entrance of woman to new fields of labour is based more or less instinctively on the fear of personal loss, there is undoubtedly a small, if a very small, number of sincere persons whose fear as to severance between the sexes to result from woman's entrance into the new field, is based upon a more abstract and impersonal ground.

It is not easy to do full justice in an exact statement to views held generally rather nebulously and vaguely, but we believe we should not mistake this view, by saying that there are a certain class of perfectly sincere and even moderately intelligent folk who hold a view which, expressed exactly, would come to something like this—that the entrance of woman into new fields would necessitate so large a mental culture and such a development of activity, mental and physical, in the woman, that she might ultimately develop into a being so superior to the male and so widely different from the man, that the bond of sympathy between the sexes might ultimately be broken and the man cease to be an object of affection and attraction to the woman, and the woman to the man through mere dissimilarity. The future these persons seem to see, more or less vaguely, is of a social condition, in which, the males of the race remaining precisely as they are today, the corresponding females shall have advanced to undreamed of heights of culture and intelligence; a condition in which the hand-worker, and the ordinary official, and small farmer, shall be confronted with the female astronomer or Greek professor of astonishing learning and gifts as his only possible complementary sex companion; and the

147

vision naturally awakens in these good folk certain misgivings as to sympathy between and suitability for each other, of these two widely dissimilar parts of humanity.

It must of course at once be admitted, that, were the two sexual halves of humanity distinct species, which, having once entered on a course of evolution and differentiation, might continue to develop along those distinct lines for countless ages or even for a number of generations, without reacting through inheritance on each other, the consequences of such development might ultimately almost completely sever them.

The development of distinct branches of humanity has already brought about such a severance between races and classes which are in totally distinct stages of evolution. So wide is the hiatus between them often, that the lowest form of sex attraction can hardly cross it; and the more highly developed mental and emotional sex passion cannot possibly bridge it. In the world of sex, kind seeks kind, and too wide a dissimilarity completely bars the existence of the highest forms of sex emotion, and often even the lower and more purely animal.

Were it possible to place a company of the most highly evolved human females—George Sands, Sophia Kovalevskys, or even the average cultured females of a highly evolved race—on an island where the only males were savages of the Fugean type, who should meet them on the shores with matted hair and prognathous jaws, and with wild shouts, brandishing their implements of death, to greet and welcome them, it is an undoubted fact that, so great would be the horror felt by the females towards them, that not only would the race become extinct, but if it depended for its continuance on any approach to sex affection on the part of the women, that death would certainly be accepted by all, as the lesser of two evils. Hardly less marked would be the sexual division if, in place of cultured and developed females, we imagine males of the same highly evolved class thrown into contact with the lowest form of primitive females. A Darwin, a Schiller, a Keats, though all men capable of

148

the strongest sex emotion and of the most durable sex affections, would probably be untouched by any emotion but horror, cast into the company of a circle of Bushmen females with greased bodies and twinkling eyes, devouring the raw entrails of slaughtered beasts.

But leaving out even such extreme instances of diversity, the mere division in culture and mental habits, dividing individuals of the same race but of different classes, tends largely to exclude the possibility of at least the nobler and more enduring forms of sex emotion. The highly cultured denizen of a modern society, though he may enter into passing and temporary and animal relations with the uncultured peasant or woman of the street, seldom finds awakened within him in such cases the depth of emotion and sympathy which is necessary for the enjoyment of the closer tie of conjugal life; and it may be doubted whether the highest, most permanent, and intimate forms of sexual affection ever exist except among humans very largely identical in tastes, habits of thought, and moral and physical education. (In Greece at a certain period (as we have before noted) there does appear to have been a temporary advance of the male, so far in advance of the female as to make the difference between them almost immeasurable; but he quickly fell back to the level of the woman.) Were it possible that the entrance of woman into the new fields of labour should produce any increased divergence between man and woman in ideals, culture, or tastes, there would undoubtedly be a dangerous responsibility incurred by any who fostered such a movement.

But the most superficial study of human life and the relation of the sexes negates such a conception.

The two sexes are not distinct species but the two halves of one whole, always acting and interacting on each other through inheritance, and reproducing and blending with each other in each generation. The human female is bound organically in two ways to the males of her society: collaterally they are her companions and the co-progenitors with her of the race; but she is also the mother of the males of each succeeding generation, bearing, shaping, and impressing her personality upon them. The males and females of each human society resemble two oxen tethered to one yoke: for a moment one may move slightly forward and the other remain stationary; but they can never move farther from each other than the length of the yoke that binds them; and they must ultimately remain stationary or move forward together. That which the women of one generation are mentally or physically, that by inheritance and education the males of the next tend to be: there can be no movement or change in one sex which will not instantly have its co-ordinating effect upon the other; the males of tomorrow are being cast in the mould of the women of today. If new ideals, new moral conceptions, new methods of action are found permeating the minds of the women of one generation, they will reappear in the ideals, moral conceptions, methods of action of the men of thirty years hence; and the idea that the males of a society can ever become permanently farther removed from its females than the individual man is from the mother who bore and reared him, is at variance with every law of human inheritance.

If, further, we turn from an abstract consideration of this supposition, and examine practically in the modern world men and women as they exist today, the irrationality of the supposition is yet more evident.

Not merely is the Woman's Movement of our age not a sporadic and abnormal growth, like a cancer bearing no organic relation to the development of the rest of the social organism, but it is essentially but one important phase of a general modification which the whole of modern life is undergoing. Further, careful study of the movement will show that, not only is it not a movement on the part of woman leading to severance and separation between the woman and the man, but that it is essentially a movement of the woman towards the man, of the sexes towards closer union.

Much is said at the present day on the subject of the "New

Woman" (who, as we have seen, is essentially but the old non-parasitic woman of the remote past, preparing to draw on her new twentieth-century garb): and it cannot truly be said that her attitude finds a lack of social attention. On every hand she is examined, praised, blamed, mistaken for her counterfeit, ridiculed, or deified—but nowhere can it be said, that the phenomenon of her existence is overlooked.

But there exists at the present day another body of social phenomena, quite as important, as radical, and if possible more far-reaching in its effects on the present and future, which yet attracts little conscious attention or animadversion, though it makes itself everywhere felt; as the shade of a growing tree may be sat under year after year by persons who never remark its silent growth.

Side by side with the "New Woman," corresponding to her, as the two sides of a coin cast in one mould, though differing from each other in superficial detail, are yet of one metal, one size, and one value; old in the sense in which she is old, being merely the reincarnation under the pressure of new conditions of the ancient forms of his race; new in the sense in which she is new, in that he is an adaptation to material and social conditions which have no exact counterpart in the past; more diverse from his immediate progenitors than even the woman is from hers, side by side with her today in every society and in every class in which she is found, stands—the New Man!

If it be asked, How comes it to pass, if, under the pressure of social conditions, man shows an analogous change of attitude toward life, that the change in woman should attract universal attention, while the corresponding change in the man of her society passes almost unnoticed?—it would seem that the explanation lies in the fact that, owing to woman's less independence of action in the past, any attempt at change or readaptation on her part has had to overcome greater resistance, and it is the noise and friction of resistance, more than the amount of actual change which has taken place, which attracts attention; as when an Alpine stream, after a long winter frost, breaks the ice, and with a crash and roar sweeps away the obstructions which have gathered in its bed, all men's attention is attracted to it, though when later a much larger body of water silently forces its way down, no man observes it. (An interesting practical illustration of this fact is found in the vast attention and uproar created when the first three women in England, some thirty odd years ago, sought to enter the medical profession. At the present day scores of women prepare to enter it yearly without attracting any general attention; not that the change which is going on is not far more in volume and social importance, but that, having overcome the first obstruction, it is now noiseless.)

Between the Emilias and Sophy Westerns of a bygone generation and the most typical of modern women, there exists no greater gap (probably not so great a one) as that which exists between the Tom Joneses and Squire Westerns of that day and the most typical of entirely modern men.

The sexual and social ideals which dominated the fox-hunting, hard-drinking, high-playing, recklessly loose-living country squire, clergyman, lawyer, and politician who headed the social organism of the past, are at least as distinct from the ideals which dominate thousands of their male descendants holding corresponding positions in the societies of today, as are the ideals of her great-great-grand mother's remote from those dominating the most modern of New Women.

That which most forces itself upon us as the result of a close personal study of those sections of modern European societies in which change and adaptation to the new conditions of life are now most rapidly progressing, is, not merely that equally large bodies of men and women are being rapidly modified as to their sexual and social ideals and as to their mode of life, but that this change is strictly complementary.

If the ideal of the modern woman becomes increasingly one inconsistent with the passive existence of woman on the remuneration which her sexual attributes may win from man, and marriage becomes for her increasingly a fellowship of comrades, rather than the relationship of the owner and the bought, the keeper and the kept; the ideal of the typically modern man departs quite as strongly from that of his forefathers in the direction of finding in woman active companionship and co-operation rather than passive submission. If the New Woman's conception of parenthood differs from the old in the greater sense of the gravity and obligation resting on those who are responsible for the production of the individual life, making her attitude toward the production of her race widely unlike the reckless, unreasoning, maternal reproduction of the woman of the past, the most typical male tends to feel in at least the same degree the moral and social obligation entailed by awakening lifehood: if the ideal which the New Woman shapes for herself of a male companion excludes the crudely animal hard-drinking, hard-swearing, licentious, even if materially wealthy gallant of the past; the most typically modern male's ideal for himself excludes at least equally this type. The brothel, the race-course, the gaming-table, and habits of physical excess among men are still with us; but the most superficial study of our societies will show that these have fallen into a new place in the scale of social institutions and manners. The politician, the clergyman, or the lawyer does not improve his social or public standing by violent addictions in these directions; to drink his companions under the table, to be known to have the largest number of illicit sex relations, to be recognised as an habitual visitant of the gambling saloon, does not, even in the case of a crowned head, much enhance his reputation, and with the ordinary man may ultimately prove a bar to all success. If the New Woman's conception of love between the sexes is one more largely psychic and intellectual than crudely and purely physical, and wholly of an affection between companions; the New Man's conception as expressed in the most typical literature and art, produced by typically modern males, gives voice with a force no woman has surpassed to the same new ideal. If to the typical modern woman the lifelong companionship of a Tom Jones or Squire Western would be more intolerable than death or the most complete celibacy, not less would the most typical of modern men shrink from the prospect of a lifelong fetterment to the companionship of an always fainting, weeping, and terrified Emilia or a Sophia of a bygone epoch.

If anywhere on earth exists the perfect ideal of that which the modern woman desires to be—of a labouring and virile womanhood, free, strong, fearless and tender—it will probably be found imaged in the heart of the New Man; engendered there by his own highest needs and aspirations; and nowhere would the most highly developed modern male find an image of that which forms his ideal of the most fully developed manhood, than in the ideal of man which haunts the heart of the New Woman.

Those have strangely overlooked some of the most important phenomena of our modern world, who see in the Woman's Movement of our day any emotional movement of the female against the male, of the woman away from the man.

We have called the Woman's Movement of our age an endeavour on the part of women among modern civilised races to find new fields of labour as the old slip from them, as an attempt to escape from parasitism and an inactive dependence upon sex function alone; but, viewed from another side, the Woman's Movement might not less justly be called a part of a great movement of the sexes towards each other, a movement towards common occupations, common interests, common ideals, and towards an emotional sympathy between the sexes more deeply founded and more indestructible than any the world has yet seen.

But it may be suggested, and the perception of a certain profound truth underlies this suggestion; How is it, if there be this close reciprocity between the lines along which the advanced and typical modern males and females are developing, that there does exist in our modern societies, and often among the very classes forming our typically advanced sections, so much of pain, unrest, and sexual disco-ordination at the present day?

The reply to this pertinent suggestion is, that the disco-ordination, struggle, and consequent suffering which undoubtedly do exist when we regard the world of sexual relationships and ideals in our modern societies, do not arise in any way from a disco-ordination between the sexes as such, but are a part of the general upheaval, of the conflict between old ideals and new; a struggle which is going on in every branch the human life in our modern societies, and in which the determining element is not sex, but the point of evolution which the race or the individual has reached.

It cannot be too often repeated, even at the risk of the most wearisome reiteration, that our societies are societies in a state of rapid evolution and change. The continually changing material conditions of life, with their reaction on the intellectual, emotional, and moral aspects of human affairs, render our societies the most complex and probably the most mobile and unsettled which the world has ever seen. As the result of this rapidity of change and complexity, there must continually exist a large amount of disco-ordination, and consequently, of suffering.

In a stationary society where generation has succeeded generation for hundreds, or it may be for thousands, of years, with little or no change in the material conditions of life, the desires, institutions, and moral principles of men, their religious, political, domestic, and sexual institutions, have gradually shaped themselves in accordance with these conditions; and a certain harmony, and homogeneity, and tranquillity, pervades the society.

In societies in that rapid state of change in which our modern societies find themselves, where not merely each decade, but each year, and almost day brings new forces and conditions to bear on life, not only is the amount of suffering and social rupture, which all rapid, excessive, and sudden change entails on an organism, inevitable; but, the new conditions, acting at different angles of intensity on the different individual members composing the society, according to their positions and varying intelligence, are producing a society of such marvellous complexity and dissimilarity in the different individual parts, that the intensest rupture and disco-ordination between individuals is inevitable; and sexual ideals and relationships must share in the universal condition.

In a primitive society (if a somewhat prolix illustration may be allowed) where for countless generations the conditions of life had remained absolutely unchanged; where for ages it had been necessary that all males should employ themselves in subduing wild beasts and meeting dangerous foes, polygamy might universally have been a necessity, if the race were to exist and its numbers be kept up; and society, recognising this, polygamy would be an institution universally approved and submitted to, however much suffering it entailed. If food were scarce, the destruction of superfluous infants and of the aged might also always have been necessary for the good of the individuals themselves as well as of society, and the whole society would acquiesce in it without any moral doubt. If an eclipse of the sun had once occurred in connection with the appearance of a certain new insect, they mighty universally regard that insect as a god causing it; and ages might pass without anything arising to disprove their belief. There would be no social or religious problem; and the view of one man would be the view of all men; and all would be more or less in harmony with the established institution and customs.

But, supposing the sudden arrival of strangers armed with superior weapons and knowledge, who should exterminate all wild beasts and render war and the consequent loss of male life a thing of the past; not only would the male be driven to encroach on the female's domain of domestic agriculture and labour generally, but the males, not being so largely destroyed, they would soon equal and surpass in numbers the females; and not only would it then become a moot matter, "a problem," which labours were or were not to be performed by man and which by woman, but very soon, not the woman alone nor the man alone, but both, would be driven to speculate as to the desirability or necessity of polygamy, which, were men as numerous as women, would leave many males without sex companions. The more intelligent and progressive individuals in the community would almost at once arrive at the conclusion that polygamy was objectionable; the most fearless would seek to carry their theory into action; the most ignorant and unprogressive would determinately stick to the old institutions as inherited from the past, without reason or question; differences of ideal would cause conflict and dissension in all parts of the body social, and suffering would ensue, where all before was fixed and determinate. So also if the strangers introduced new and improved methods of agriculture, and food became abundant, it would then at once strike the most far-seeing and readily adaptable members of the community, both male and female, that there was no necessity for the destruction of their offspring; old men and women would begin seriously to object to being hastened to death when they realised that starvation did not necessarily stare them in the face if they survived to an extreme old age; the most stupid and hide-bound members of the community would still continue to sacrifice parents and offspring long after the necessity had ceased, under the influence of traditional bias; many persons would be in a state of much moral doubt as to which course of action to pursue, the old or the new; and bitter conflict might rage in the community on all these points. Were the strangers to bring with them telescopes, looking through which it might at once clearly be seen that an eclipse of the sun was caused merely by the moon's passing over its face, the more intelligent members of the community would at once come to the conclusion that the insect was not the cause of eclipses, would cease to regard it as a god, and might even kill it; the more stupid and immobile section of the community might refuse to look through the telescope, or looking might refuse to see that it was the moon which caused the eclipse, and their deep-seated reverence for the insect, which was the growth of ages, would lead them to regard as impious those individuals who denied its godhead, and might even lead to the physical destruction of the first unbelievers. The society, once so homogeneous and co-ordinated in all its parts, would become at once a society rent by moral and social problems; and endless suffering must arise to individuals in the attempt to co-ordinate the ideals, manners, and institutions of the society to the new conditions! There might be immense gain in many directions; lives otherwise sacrificed would be spared, a higher and more satisfactory stage of existence might be entered on; but the disco-ordination and struggle would be inevitable until the society had established an equilibrium between its knowledge, its material conditions, and its social, sexual, and religious ideals and institutions.

An analogous condition, but of a far more complex kind, exists at the present day in our own societies. Our material environment differs in every respect from that of our grandparents, and bears little or no resemblance to that of a few centuries ago. Here and there, even in our civilised societies in remote agricultural districts, the old social conditions may remain partly undisturbed; but throughout the bulk of our societies the substitution of mechanical for hand-labour, the wide diffusion of knowledge through the always increasing cheap printing-press; the rapidly increasing gathering of human creatures into vast cities, where not merely thousands but millions of individuals are collected together under physical and mental conditions of life which invert every social condition of the past; the increasingly rapid means of locomotion; the increasing intercourse between distant races and lands, brought about by rapid means of intercommunication, widening and changing in every direction the human horizon—all these produce a society, so complex and so rapidly altering, that social co-ordination between all its parts is impossible; and social unrest, and the strife of ideals of faiths, of institutions, and consequent human suffering is inevitable.

If the ancient guns and agricultural implements which our fathers taught us to use are valueless in the hands of their descendants, if the samplers our mothers worked and the stockings they knitted are become superfluous through the action of the modern loom, yet more are their social institutions, faiths, and manners of life become daily and increasingly unfitted to our use; and friction and suffering inevitable, especially for the most advanced and modified individuals in our societies. This suffering, if we analyse it closely, rises from three causes.

Firstly, it is caused by the fact that mere excessive rapidity of change tends always easily to become painful, by rupturing violently already hardened habits and modes of thought, as a very rapidly growing tree ruptures its bark and exudes its internal juices.

Secondly, it arises from the fact that individuals of the same human society, not adapting themselves at the same rate to the new conditions, or being exposed to them in different degrees, a wide and almost unparalleled dissimilarity has today arisen between the different individuals composing our societies; where, side by side with men and women who have rapidly adapted or are so successfully seeking to adapt themselves to the new conditions of knowledge and new conditions of life, that, were they to reappear in future ages in more co-ordinated societies, they might perhaps hardly appear wholly antiquated, are to be found men and women whose social, religious, and moral ideals would not constitute them out of harmony if returned to the primitive camps of the remote forbears of the human race; while, between these extreme classes lies that large mass of persons in an intermediate state of development. This diversity is bound to cause friction and suffering in the interactions of the members of our societies; more especially, as the individuals composing each type are not sorted out into classes and families, but are found scattered through all classes and grades in our societies. (One of the women holding the most advanced and modern view of the relation of woman to life whom we have met was the wife of a Northamptonshire shoemaker; herself engaged in making her living by the sewing of the uppers of men's boots.) Persons bound by the closest ties of blood or social contiguity and compelled to a continual intercourse, are often those most widely dissevered in their amount of adaptation to the new conditions of life; and the amount of social friction and consequent human suffering arising from this fact is so subtle and almost incalculable, that perhaps it is impossible adequately to portray it in dry didactic language: it is only truly describable in the medium of art, where actual concrete individuals are shown acting and reacting on each other—as in the novel or the drama. We are like a company of chess-men, not sorted out in kinds, pawns together, kings and queens together, and knights and rooks together, but simply thrown at haphazard into a box, and jumbled side by side. In the stationary societies, where all individuals were permeated by the same political, religious, moral, and social ideas; and where each class had its own hereditary and fixed traditions of action and manners, this cause of friction and suffering had of necessity no existence; individual differences and discord might be occasioned by personal greeds, ambitions, and selfishnesses, but not by conflicting conceptions of right and wrong, of the desirable and undesirable, in all branches of human life. (Only those who have been thrown into contact with a stationary and homogeneous society such as that of primitive African tribes before coming in contact with Europeans; or such as the up-country Boers of South Africa were twenty years ago, can realise adequately how wholly free from moral and social problems and social friction such a society can be. It is in studying such societies that the truth is vividly forced on one, that the key to half, and more than half, of the phenomena in our own social condition, can be found only in our rapidly changing conditions necessitating equally rapid change in our conceptions, ideals, and institutions.)

Thirdly, the unrest and suffering peculiar to our age is caused by conflict going on within the individual himself. So intensely rapid is the change which is taking place in our environment and knowledge that in the course of a single life a man may pass through half a dozen phases of growth. Born and reared in possession of certain ideas and manners of action, he or she may, before middle life is reached, have had occasion repeatedly to modify, enlarge, and alter, or completely throw aside those traditions. Within the individuality itself of such persons, goes on, in an intensified form, that very struggle, conflict, and disco-ordination which is going on in society at large between its different members and sections; and agonising moments must arise, when the individual, seeing the necessity for adopting new courses of action, or for accepting new truths, or conforming to new conditions, will yet be tortured by the hold of traditional convictions; and the man or woman who attempts to adapt their life to the new material conditions and to harmony with the new knowledge, is almost bound at some time to rupture the continuity of their own psychological existence.

It is these conditions which give rise to the fact so often noticed, that the art of our age tends persistently to deal with subtle social problems, religious, political, and sexual, to which the art of the past holds no parallel; and it is so inevitably, because the artist who would obey the artistic instinct to portray faithfully the world about him, must portray that which lies at the core of its life. The "problem" play, novel, and poem are as inevitable in this age, as it was inevitable that the artist of the eleventh century should portray tournaments, physical battles, and chivalry, because they were the dominant element in the life about him.

It is also inevitable that this suffering and conflict must make itself felt in its acutest form in the person of the most advanced individual of our societies. It is the swimmer who first leaps into the frozen stream who is cut sharpest by the ice; those who follow him find it broken, and the last find it gone. It is the man or woman who first treads down the path which the bulk of humanity will ultimately follow, who must find themselves at last in solitudes where the silence is deadly. The fact that any course of human action leading to adjustment, leads also to immediate suffering, by dividing the individual from the bulk of his fellows; is no argument against it; that solitude and suffering is the crown of thorns which marks the kingship of earth's Messiahs: it is the mark of the leader.

Thus, social disco-ordination, and subjective conflict and suffering, pervade the life of our age, making themselves felt in every division of human life, religious, political, and domestic; and, if they are more noticeable, and make themselves more keenly felt in the region of sex than in any other, even the religious, it is because when we enter the region of sex we touch, as it were, the spinal cord of human existence, its great nerve centre, where sensation is most acute, and pain and pleasure most keenly felt. It is not sex disco-ordination that is at the root of our social unrest; it is the universal disco-ordination which affects even the world of sex phenomena.

Also it is necessary to note that the line which divides the progressive sections of our communities, seeking to co-ordinate themselves to the new conditions of life, from the retrogressive, is not a line running coincidentally with the line of sex. A George Sand and a Henrik Ibsen belong more essentially to the same class in the order of modern development, than either belongs to any class composed entirely of their own sex. If we divide humanity into classes according to type, in each division will be found the male with his complementary female. Side by side with the old harlot at the street corner anxious to sell herself, stands the old aboriginal male, whether covered or not with a veneer of civilisation, eager and desiring to buy. Side by side with the parasitic woman, seeking only increased pleasure and luxury from her relations with man, stands the male seeking only pleasure and self-indulgence from his relations with her. Side by side with the New Woman, anxious for labour and seeking from man only such love and fellowship as she gives, stands the New Man, anxious to possess her only on the terms she offers. If the social movement, through which the most advanced women of our day are attempting to bring themselves into co-ordination with the new conditions of life, removes them immeasurably from certain types of the primitive male; the same movement equally removes the new male from the old female. The sexual tragedy of modern life lies, not in the fact that woman as such is tending to differ fundamentally from man as such; but that, in the unassorted confusion of our modern life, it is continually the modified type of man or woman who is thrown into the closest personal relations with the antiquated type of the opposite sex; that between father and daughter, mother and son, brother and sister, husband and wife, may sometimes be found to intervene not merely years, but even centuries of social evolution.

It is not man as man who opposes the attempt of woman to readjust herself to the new conditions of life: that opposition arises, perhaps more often, from the retrogressive members of her own sex. And it is a fact which will surprise no one who has studied the conditions of modern life; that among the works of literature in all European languages, which most powerfully advocate the entrance of woman into the new fields of labour, and which most uncompromisingly demand for her the widest training and freedom of action, and which most passionately seek for the breaking down of all artificial lines which sever the woman from the man, many of the ablest and most uncompromising are the works of males.

The New Man and Woman do not resemble two people, who, standing on a level plain, set out on two roads, which diverging at different angles and continued in straight lines, must continue to take them farther and farther from each other the longer they proceed in them; rather, they resemble two persons who start to climb a spur of the same mountain from opposite sides; where, the higher they climb the nearer they come to each other, being bound ultimately to meet at the top.

Even that opposition often made by males to the entrance of woman into the new fields of labour, of which they at present hold the monopoly, is not fundamentally sexual in its nature. The male who opposes the entrance of woman into the trade or profession in which he holds more or less a monopoly, would oppose with equal, and perhaps even greater bitterness, the opening of its doors to numbers of his own sex who had before been excluded, and who would limit his gains and share his privileges. It is the primitive brute instinct to retain as much as possible for the ego, irrespective of justice or humanity, which dominates all the lower moral types of humanity, both male and female, which acts here. The lawyer or physician who objects to the entrance of women to his highly fenced professional enclosure, would probably object yet more strenuously if it were proposed to throw down the barriers of restraint and monetary charges, which would result in the flooding of his profession by other males: while the mechanic, who resists the entrance of woman into his especial field, is invariably found even more persistently to oppose any attempt at entrance on the part of other males, when he finds it possible to do so.

This opposition of the smaller type of male, to the entrance of woman into the callings hitherto apportioned to himself, is sometimes taken as implying the impossibility of fellowship and affection existing between the men and women employed in common labour, that the professional jealousy of the man must necessitate his feeling a hatred and antagonism towards any one who shares his fields of toil. But the most superficial study of human life negates such a supposition. Among men, in spite of the occasional existence of the petty professional jealousies and antagonism, we find, viewing society as a whole, that common interests, and above all common labours, are the most potent means of bringing them into close and friendly relations; and, in fact, they seem generally essential for the formation of the closest and most permanent human friendships. In every walk of human life, whether trade, or profession, we find men associating by choice mainly with, and entertaining often the profoundest and most permanent friendships for, men engaged in their own callings. The inner circle of a barrister's friendships almost always consists of his fellow-barristers; the city man, who is free to select his society where he will, will be oftenest found in company with his fellow-man of business; the medical man's closest friendship is, in a large number of cases, for some man who was once his fellow-student and has passed through the different stages of his professional life with him; the friends and chosen companions of the actor are commonly actors; of the savant, savants; of the farmer, farmers; of the sailor, sailors. So generally is this the case that it would almost attract attention and cause amusement were the boon companion of the sea captain a leading politician, and the intimate friend of the clergyman an actor, or the dearest friend of the farmer an astronomer. Kind seeks kind. The majority of men by choice frequent clubs where those of their own calling are found, and especially as life advances and men sink deeper into their professional grooves, they are found to seek fellowship mainly among their fellow-workers. That this should be so is inevitable; common amusements may create a certain bond between the young, but the performance of common labours, necessitating identical knowledge, identical habits, and modes of thought, forms a far stronger bond, drawing men far more powerfully towards social intercourse and personal friendship and affection than the centrifugal force of professional jealousies can divide them.

That the same condition would prevail where women became fellow-workers with men might be inferred on abstract grounds: but practical experience confirms this. The actor oftenest marries the actress, the male musician the female; the reception-room of the literary woman or female painter is found continually frequented by men of her own calling; the woman-doctor associates continually with and often marries one of her own confreres; and as women in increasing numbers share the fields of labour with men, which have hitherto been apportioned to them alone, the nature and strength of the sympathy arising from common labours will be increasingly clear.

The sharing by men and women of the same labours, necessitating a common culture and therefore common habits of thought and interests, would tend to fill that painful hiatus which arises so continually in modern conjugal life, dividing the man and woman as soon as the first sheen of physical sexual attraction which glints only over the unknown begins to fade, and from which springs so large a part of the tragedy of modern conjugal relations. The primitive male might discuss with her his success in hunting and her success in finding roots; as the primitive peasant may discuss today with his wife the crops and cows in which both are equally interested and which both understand; there is nothing in their order of life to produce always increasingly divergent habits of thought and interest.

In modern civilised life, in many sections, the lack of any common labour and interests and the wide dissimilarity of the life led by the man and the woman, tend continually to produce increasing divergence; so that, long before middle life is reached, they are left without any bond of co-cohesion but that of habit. The comradeship and continual stimulation, rising from intercourse with those sharing our closest interests and regarding life from the same standpoint, the man tends to seek in his club and among his male companions, and the woman accepts solitude, or seeks dissipations which tend yet farther to disrupt the common conjugal life. A certain mental camaraderie and community of impersonal interests is imperative in conjugal life in addition to a purely sexual relation, if the union is to remain a living and always growing reality. It is more especially because the sharing by woman of the labours of man will tend to promote camaraderie and the existence of common, impersonal interests and like habits of thought and life, that the entrance of women into the very fields shared by men, and not into others peculiarly reserved for her, is so desirable. (The reply once given by the wife of a leading barrister, when reference was made to the fact that she and her husband were seldom found in each other's society, throws a painful but true light on certain aspects of modern life, against which the entire woman's movement of our age is a rebellion. "My husband," she said, "is always increasingly absorbed in his legal duties, of which I understand nothing, and which so do not interest me. My children are all growing up and at school. I have servants enough to attend to my house. When he comes home in the evening, if I try to amuse him by telling him of the things I have been doing during the day, of the bazaars I am working for, the shopping I have done, the visits I have paid, he is bored. He is anxious to get away to his study, his books, and his men friends, and I am left utterly alone. If it were not for the society of women and other men with whom I have more in common, I could not bear my life. When we first met as boy and girl, and fell in love, we danced and rode together and seemed to have everything in common; now we have nothing. I respect him and I believe he respects me, but that is all!" It is, perhaps, only in close confidences between man and man and woman and woman that this open sore, rising from the divergence in training, habits of life, and occupation between men and women is spoken of; but it lies as a tragic element at the core of millions of modern conjugal relations, beneath the smooth superficial surface of our modern life; breaking out to the surface only occasionally in the revelations of our divorce courts.)

It is a gracious fact, to which every woman who has achieved success or accomplished good work in any of the fields generally apportioned to men will bear witness, whether that work be in the field of literature, of science, or the organised professions, that the hands which have been most eagerly stretched our to welcome her have been those of men; that the voices which have most generously acclaimed her success have been those of male fellow-workers in the fields into which she has entered.

There is no door at which the hand of woman has knocked for admission into a new field of toil but there have been found on the other side the hands of strong and generous men eager to turn it for her, almost before she knocks.

To those of us who, at the beginning of a new century, stand with shaded eyes, gazing into the future, striving to descry the outlines of the shadowy figures which loom before us in the distance, nothing seems of so gracious a promise, as the outline we seem to discern of a condition of human life in which a closer union than the world has yet seen shall exist between the man and the woman: where the Walhalla of our old Northern ancestors shall find its realisation in a concrete reality, and the Walkurie and her hero feast together at one board, in a brave fellowship.

Always in our dreams we hear the turn of the key that shall close the door of the last brothel; the clink of the last coin that pays for the body and soul of a woman; the falling of the last wall that encloses artificially the activity of woman and divides her from man; always we picture the love of the sexes, as, once a dull, slow, creeping worm; then a torpid, earthy chrysalis; at last the full-winged insect, glorious in the sunshine of the future.

Today, as we row hard against the stream of life, is it only a blindness in our eyes, which have been too long strained, which makes us see, far up the river where it fades into the distance, through all the mists that rise from the river-banks, a clear, a golden light? Is it only a delusion of the eyes which makes us grasp our oars more lightly and bend our backs lower; though we know well that long before the boat reaches those stretches, other hands than ours will man the oars and guide its helm? Is it all a dream?

The ancient Chaldean seer had a vision of a Garden of Eden which lay in a remote past. It was dreamed that man and woman once lived in joy and fellowship, till woman ate of the tree of knowledge and gave to man to eat; and that both were driven forth to wander, to toil in bitterness; because they had eaten of the fruit.

We also have our dream of a Garden: but it lies in a distant future. We dream that woman shall eat of the tree of knowledge together with man, and that side by side and hand close to hand, through ages of much toil and labour, they shall together raise about them an Eden nobler than any the Chaldean dreamed of; an Eden created by their own labour and made beautiful by their own fellowship.

In his apocalypse there was one who saw a new heaven and a new earth; we see a new earth; but therein dwells love—the love of comrades and co-workers.

It is because so wide and gracious to us are the possibilities of the future; so impossible is a return to the past, so deadly is a passive acquiescence in the present, that today we are found everywhere raising our strange new cry—"Labour and the training that fits us for labour!"

www.ingramcontent.com/pod-product-compliance
Lightning Source LLC
Chambersburg PA
CBHW031434270326
41930CB00007B/701